The Essential Book of
BOAT DRINKS
& Assorted Frozen Concoctions

To Fred and Fred

Other books by
Olaf Nordstrom
include
THE MARGARITAVILLE™ COOKBOOK,
THE ESSENTIAL BOOK OF TEQUILA,
and
THINGS YOU KNOW BY HEART:
1001 Questions from the Songs of Jimmy Buffett

FIFTH EDITION

The Essential Book of
BOAT DRINKS
& Assorted Frozen Concoctions

OLAF NORDSTROM

The Peninsula Press

Cape Cod, Nantucket & Martha's Vineyard

Library of Congress Catalog Card Number: 05-070316
Nordstrom, Olaf.
  The Essential Book of BOAT DRINKS & Assorted Frozen Concoctions
  The Peninsula Press, ©2009.
  ISBN 1-883684-47-1

First published in 1997

Fifth Edition
Manufactured in the United States of America
1 2 3 4 5 6 7 8 9 / 16 15 14 13 12 11 10 09 08

Contents

A Blender History Lesson

ONE EVENING BACK IN 1936, a visionary named Fred
Osius put on his dark blue woolen shirt, some striped pants,
a bright parrot-yellow tie, and a cutaway coat, then headed for
Manhattan's Vanderbilt Hotel, where a musician named Fred
Waring had just signed-off from a regular radio broadcast with his
popular singing group, the "Pennsylvanians."

Mr. Waring was backstage when the colorful Mr. Osius appeared
with the prototype of a gizmo he claimed would "revolutionize
people's eating habits." The inventor had come to ask the successful
entertainer to invest in both the making and the marketing of this
thing he called the "Miracle Mixer."

But when Fred Osius turned it on, it simply didn't work, and
he left the same way he had come in.

Undaunted, Osius spent the next six months and some $25,000
more without any further success. Meanwhile, Fred Waring
remained intrigued and eventually became interested; he liked this
guy and his idea, so he joined up with the project. By September of
1937, Fred Osius and Fred Waring had a working model for the
National Restaurant Show in Chicago. And the crowd loved it.

Soon Fred Waring was hyping the machine on the radio with a
singing group called the "Waring Blendors." A teetotaler himself,
Waring kept one in his dressing room to make juices from fruits
and vegetables. And though the two Freds had first viewed the
invention as a food mixer, the folks at the Ron Rico Rum Company
looked upon it as a machine for mixing some rather spectacular

drinks. Before long, homemakers were eager to have this new appliance in their kitchens, and nearly every bar and restaurant was becoming equipped with a Waring Blendor.

Thanks Fred, both of you. You can rest assured that your efforts have not been wasted.

FOREWORD

SINCE THIS LITTLE VOLUME was first put together for Jimmy back in the 1990s, a lot of diluted ice has coursed through my bilge, along with bits of citrus that have long since drifted out into the Gulf Stream. In the meantime, *This Honky's Dory* went to the bottom one dark and stormy night, only to have *Victorious Egret* appear in the offing a few days later. And when no one seemed to be paying much attention, Crab Key somehow became a tourist trap: a t-shirt shop, an ice cream stand, and a miniature golf course (with its own waterfall) distracted a good many travelers who were otherwise just heading south along U.S. 1. To me, that only meant it was time to light out for the territory before they try to "sivilize" me. So, these days I gaze at the sunsets from the fantail of *Victorious Egret* and reassure friends and strangers all along the eastern seaboard, "It must be two bells, somewhere!"

With that, let me welcome you once more aboard this wonderful world of blenders and shakers, of slings and fizzes, and of tall drinks and short stories: all served best with those songs that we know by heart. As every Parrothead knows, you don't need to own a boat in order to enjoy a boat drink. In fact, you don't even need to know what to call those little, round windows or that pointy end at the front of the vessel.

All you really need to understand is that this pace of life has no demand either for anything mixed with an energy drink, or anything that must be tossed back all at once in a single shot without any sense of taste or of simple conversation. And just as important, this is a place where a Margarita is a Margarita, a Martini is a Martini, and never the twain shall meet. Never trust anyone who asks for any other drink with some hybrid name that ends in "rita" or "tini." Chances are, they are the same kind of people who believe there's such a thing as a "Mexican pizza" or an "Italian taco." *Ugh!*

That is not to say that you will enjoy each and every one of the drinks in this essential little volume. Quite frankly, I can admit to you that I don't. (Do you want to highlight that sentence?) Nonetheless, I have had others ask me for these things by name or by ingredients, and I have witnessed these very same people fully imbibe whatever concoction they ordered. And live long enough to order up another. It's all a matter of taste.

So, fill up your ice bucket, wipe out your drinking glass, and put on some Buffett tunes. It is, after all, probably two bells somewhere, and we ought to sit down and drink things over.

Olaf Nordstrom
24.33° N   81.48° W / 01 March 09
Same Spot / Different Day

FOREWORD

F ICTION OVER FACT alway gets my vote," sings Jimmy Buffett in one of his lyrics, but he usually makes it tough for us to separate one from the other. Keep in mind, for instance, that his best-selling *Tales from Margaritaville* carries the subtitle of *Fictional facts and factual fictions*. I think that it's safe to say that if there's a thin line between Saturday night and Sunday morning, then there's at least a very fuzzy one between Jimmy's fiction and the facts of his life.

Consider, for example, the very origin of his song called "Boat Drinks." Is there doubt that it all began in Derek Sanderson's Boston bar? And what about that incident in "Jamaica Mistaica?" It was all over the news. But should we really believe that Jimmy was strumming his six-string on his front porch swing and simply wastin' away?

Frankly, I haven't a clue, and none of such endless speculation should take away any of the endless fun out of being a Parrothead. More often than not, I suspect, such ambiguity just adds an extra dimension.

Now follow me here, because I have an important point to make.

To paraphrase one of our *Startrek* friends, "I am not a preacher, Jim, I'm a bartender!" Being a bartender, though, I do have a responsibility that must be passed along to you. It is simply this. Whether you listen to Jimmy's lyrics as fiction or as fact, the purpose of this book is to help you further appreciate drinking as neither an end (as in "Margaritaville"), nor as a means ("Why Don't We Get Drunk and Screw?"), but more as just part of an occasion, be that in some Parrothead parking lot party or some Blue Heaven rendezvous. In which case, I think I've included a drink for all occasions, and not all of them require beer, wine, or liquor. The only requirement of this kind of drinking is friendship; the basic requirement of friendship is a concern for one another's well-being.

That said, keep in mind that this book is just a guide, not the Gospel. Though the standard of measurement is the *jigger*, a shot glass which can be 1½ ounces or 2 ounces, it is only used as a unit of measure. You can taste and tinker as you please, changing proportions and adding ingredients. Other than that, this organized collection of drink recipes is based upon nothing other than the lifestyle of Jimmy Buffett's portrayed in his lyrics, be that fiction or fact. This is not a challenge to drink your way through the alphabet.

OLAF NORDSTROM
13 September 1996
Crab Key, Florida

Essential Boat Drinks
A to Z

A1A

After one sip, you'll be at the end of your road.

INGREDIENTS:
1 jigger Rhum
3 dashes 151 Proof Rhum
½ jigger Grapefruit Juice
½ jigger Cream of Coconut
Juice of ½ Lime
Lime Wedge, for garnish

PREPARATION:
Fill your shaker with ice. Add the ingredients. Shake the mix vigorously for about thirty seconds, then strain over ice into a rocks glass. Garnish with the Wedge of Lime.

ACAPULCO

After one sip, you'll need a reason to move.

INGREDIENTS:
1 jigger Rhum
¼ jigger Triple Sec
¼ jigger Lime Juice
*1 Egg White ***
¼ t. Sugar
2 Mint Sprigs, for garnish

** *Due to the slight risk of Salmonella or other food-borne illness, I always must recommend caution in consuming raw egg whites. To reduce this risk, always use only clean, fresh, grade A or AA eggs that have been properly refrigerated. Be certain that their shells have remained intact and avoid contact between the yolks or whites and the shell.*

PREPARATION:

Fill your shaker with ice and add the ingredients. Shake the mix vigorously for about thirty seconds. Strain over ice into a rocks glass. Garnish with the Sprigs of Mint.

ADAM'S CAT

After one sip, no one else will know you.

INGREDIENTS:

1 jigger Dry Vermouth
¼ jigger Yellow Chartreuse
2 dashes Orange Bitters
Orange Peel, for garnish

PREPARATION:

Fill your shaker with crushed ice and add the ingredients. Shake the mix vigorously for about thirty seconds. Strain into a chilled cocktail glass. Garnish with the Twist of Orange.

ADIOS, BOYS!

After one sip, you might be drinkin' double.

INGREDIENTS:

1 jigger Tequila
4 jiggers Tomato Juice
½ Lime, squeezed, then dropped into the glass
Dash Tabasco

PREPARATION:
Fill your shaker with cracked ice and add only the Tequila and Tomato Juice. Shake the mix vigorously for about thirty seconds. Strain into a highball glass. Squeeze the Lime into the drink and add the Tabasco.

ADMIRAL

After one sip. you'll be sending the old man home.

INGREDIENTS:
½ jigger Bourbon
1 jigger Dry Vermouth
¼ jigger Lemon Juice
Lemon Peel, for garnish

PREPARATION:
Fill your shaker with ice, then add the ingredients. Shake the mix vigorously for about thirty seconds. Strain over ice into a rocks glass. Garnish with the Twisr of Lemon.

AFRICAN PARAKEET

After one sip, you'll open up your trusty old mind.

INGREDIENTS:
1 jigger Blackberry Brandy
½ jigger Port
½ jigger Brandy
Orange Slice, for garnish

PREPARATION:
Fill your shaker with cracked ice and add ingredients. Shake the mix vigorously for about thirty seconds. Strain into a chilled cocktail glass. Garnish with the Slice of Orange.

AFTERNOON GOLFER

After one sip, you'll be happy that you never got Rolfed.

INGREDIENTS:
2 jiggers Gin
1 jigger Dry Vermouth
2 dashes Angostura Bitters
Green Olive, for garnish

PREPARATION:
Fill your bar glass with shaved ice and add ingredients. Stir together gently, then strain into a chilled cocktail glass. Garnish with the Green Olive.

AGATHA CHRISTIE

After one sip, your life will suddenly seem a mystery.

INGREDIENTS:
1 jigger Sherry
1 jigger Dry Vermouth
1 dash Orange Bitters
Lemon Peel, for garnish

PREPARATION:
Fill your shaker with crushed ice. Add the Sherry, Dry Vermouth, and Bitters. Shake the mix vigorously for about thirty seconds. Strain into a chillded cocktail glass. Garnish with the Twist of Lemon.

ALABAMA

After one sip, you'll wish you had a Mobile home.

INGREDIENTS:
1 jigger Brandy
1 jigger Curaçao
¼ jigger Lime Juice

1 t. Simple Syrup*
Orange Peel, for garnish

* A recipe for preparing a Simple Syrup can be found in the Glossary.

PREPARATION:
Fill your shaker with ice and add ingredients. Shake the mix vigorously for about thirty seconds. Strain over ice into a rocks glass. Garnish with the Twist of Orange.

ALABAMA SLAMMER

After one sip, you'll find that the stars aren't all that falls.

INGREDIENTS:
½ jigger Sloe Gin
½ jigger Southern Comfort
½ jigger Triple Sec
½ jigger Galliano
2 jiggers Orange Juice
Orange Slice, for garnish
Cherry, for garnish

PREPARATION:
Fill your shaker with ice, then add together only the first five ingredients. Shake the mix vigorously for about thirty seconds. Strain over ice into a collins glass. Garnish with the Cherry and the Slice of Orange.

ALTERED BOY

After one sip, you'll be doing it just because you can.

INGREDIENTS:
½ jigger Light Rhum
½ jigger Dry Vermouth
1 jigger Lime Juice

3 dashes Triple Sec
3 dashes Grenadine
Orange Slice, for garnish

PREPARATION:
Fill your shaker with crushed ice. Add the ingredients.
Shake the mix vigorously for about thirty seconds. Strain
into a chilled cocktail glass. Garnish with the Slice of
Orange.

APOCALIPS

After one sip, you'll have trouble just moving your own.

INGREDIENTS:
2 jigger Gin
1 jigger Galliano
½ jigger Crème de Banana
1 jigger Grapefruit Juice

PREPARATION:
Fill your shaker with ice and add ingredients. Shake the
mix vigorously for about thirty seconds. Strain into a
chilled cocktail glass.

AROUND THE WORLD

After one sip, you'll start reciting departure signs from some
forgotten ports.

INGREDIENTS:
1 jigger Gin
1 jigger Crème de Menthe
1 jigger Pineapple Juice
¼ Pineapple Slice, for garnish

PREPARATION:
Fill your shaker with ice and add together the Gin, Crème
de Menthe, and Pineapple Juice. Shake the mix vigorously

for about thirty seconds. Strain over ice into a rocks glass. Garnish with Slice of Pineapple.

Atlantic Breeze

After one sip, you'll be gone with the wind.

INGREDIENTS:
> *1 jigger Light Rum*
> *½ jigger Apricot Brandy*
> *2 jiggers Pineapple Juice*
> *½ jigger Lemon Juice*
> *½ jigger Galliano*
> *Dash Grenadine*
> *Cherry, for garnish*
> *Orange Slice, for garnish*

PREPARATION:
> Fill your shaker with ice and add together the ingredients. Shake the mix vigorously for about thirty seconds. Strain over ice into a collins glass. Garnish with the Cherry and the Slice of Orange.

Attitude Change

After one sip, nothing remains quite the same.

INGREDIENTS:
> *1 jigger Light Rhum*
> *½ jigger Kahlúa*
> *½ jigger White Crème de Cacao*
> *2 dashes Curaçao*

PREPARATION:
> Fill your shaker with ice and add together the ingredients. Shake the mix vigorously for about thirty seconds. Strain over ice into a rocks glass.

- B -

BAD HABIT

After one sip, you'll find the price of vice foretold.

INGREDIENTS:

½ jigger Light Rhum
½ jigger Coconut Rhum
¼ jigger Spiced Rhum
¼ jigger Vodka
½ jigger Gin
1 jigger Sour Mix*
1 t. Powdered Sugar
Dash bitters
2 dashes Grenadine
Soda Water
Pineapple Wedge, for garnish

* A recipe for preparing a Sour Mix can be found in the Glossary.

PREPARATION:

Fill your blender about one-quarter with cracked ice. Add the first nine ingredients. Blend on high for about thirty seconds and strain over ice into a rocks glass. Fill with Soda Water, then swizzle gently. Garnish with the Pineapple Wedge.

BAHAMA MAMA

After one sip, you'll drop anchor in another particular harbor.

INGREDIENTS:
1 jigger Light Rhum
1 jigger Dark Rhum
½ jigger Cream of Coconut
2 jiggers Pineapple Juice
1 jigger Orange Juice
Cherry, for garnish
¼ Pineapple Slice, for garnish

PREPARATION:
Fill your blender one-quarter with ice. Add ingredients. Blend for only thirty seconds, then pour into a frosted collins glass. Garnish with the Cherry and the Slice of Pineapple.

BAMA BREEZE

After one sip, you'll feel at home down there.

INGREDIENTS:
1 jigger Amaretto
1 jigger Southern Comfort
1 jigger Sloe Gin
Orange Juice
Orange Slice, for garnish

PREPARATION:
Fill your shaker with ice. Add the Amaretto, Southern Comfort, and Sloe Gin. Shake the mix vigorously for about thirty seconds. Strain over ice into a collins glass. Fill with Orange Juice. Swizzle once or twice. Garnish with the Slice of Orange.

BAMBOO

After one sip, you'll forget that it's a jungle out there.

INGREDIENTS:

1½ jiggers Jamaican Rhum
Cola
Dash Orange Bitters
Orange Peel, for garnish

PREPARATION:

Fill a highball glass with ice and add the Rhum. Fill with Cola, then splash with the Orange Bitters. Swizzle gently, then garnish with the Twist of Orange.

BANANA MAMA

After one sip, you'll find that everyone has a peel.

INGREDIENTS:

1 jigger Light Rhum
½ jigger Dark Rhum
½ jigger Banana Liqueur
½ jigger Cream of Coconut
1 oz. Strawberries, fresh or frozen
1 jigger Pineapple Juice

PREPARATION:

Fill your blender one-quarter with crushed ice. Add in all of the ingredients. Blend about a minute or until smooth, then pour into a frosted goblet.

BANANA REPUBLICAN

After one sip, you'll probably want to (g.o.) p—.

INGREDIENTS:

1 jigger Gold Rhum
1 jigger Crème de Banana

½ *jigger Dark Rhum*
½ *jigger Curaçao*
¼ *jigger Grenadine*
Juice of 1 Lime
Lime Peel, for garnish

PREPARATION:
Fill your shaker with crushed ice. Add in only the liquid ingredients. Shake the mix vigorously for about thirty seconds. Strain into a frosted cocktail glass. Garnish with the Twist of Lime.

BANANA WIND

After one sip, you'll forget you know all the lyrics.

INGREDIENTS:
  1 jigger Light Rhum
  1 jigger Crème de Banana
  1 jigger White Crème de Cacao
  2 jiggers Cream
  ½ ripened Banana
  Cherry, for garnish
  Wedge of Pineapple, for garnish

PREPARATION:
Fill your blender one-quarter with ice. Add the first five ingredients. Blend about a minute or until smooth, then pour into a frosted goblet. Garnish with the Cherry and the Pineapple Wedge.

BARBARY COAST

After one sip, you'll have a piratical nerve.

INGREDIENTS:
  1 jigger Light Rhum
  1 jigger Gin

1 jigger Scotch
1 jigger Crème de Cacao
1 jigger Cream

PREPARATION:
Fill your shaker with ice. Add all the ingredients. Shake the mix vigorously for about thirty seconds. Strain into a chilled cocktail glass.

BARE-ASSED CHILD IN THE RAIN

After one sip, you'll have no need to explain.

INGREDIENTS:
1 jigger Gin
2 jiggers Sour Mix*
6 oz. Beer

* A recipe for preparing a Sour Mix can be found in the Glossary.

PREPARATION:
Fill a collins glass with ice. Add the Gin and Sour Mix. Swizzle. Fill the glass with Beer.

BAYBREEZE

After one sip, you'll think any direction it blows will be fine.

INGREDIENTS:
1 jigger Vodka
1½ jiggers Cranberry Juice
1½ jiggers Pineapple Juice

PREPARATION:
Fill your shaker with ice. Add the three ingredients. Shake the mix vigorously for about thirty seconds. Strain into a chilled cocktail glass.

BEACHCOMBER

After one sip, you'll have a style of your own.

INGREDIENTS:
1 ½ jiggers Light Rhum
½ jigger Cointreau
Juice of ½ Lime
2 dashes Maraschino Liqueur
Cherry, for garnish

PREPARATION:
Fill your shaker with ice. Add the ingredients. Shake the mix vigorously for about thirty seconds. Strain into a chilled cocktail glass. Garnish with the Cherry.

BETWEEN THE SHEETS

After one sip, you'll walk like you're "three sheets to the wind."

INGREDIENTS:
1 jigger Brandy
1 jigger Cointreau
1 jigger Light Rhum
Twist of Orange, for garnish

PREPARATION:
Fill your shaker with ice. Add the three main ingredients. Shake the mix vigorously for about thirty seconds. Strain into a cocktail glass. Garnish with the Twist of Orange.

BIG EASY

After one sip, you'll think it's Mardi Gras!

INGREDIENTS:
½ Sugar Cube
Dash Orange Bitters
2 dashes Angostura Bitters

Dash Anisette
2 dashes Pernod
1 jigger Bourbon
Lemon Twist, for garnish

PREPARATION:

Place your Sugar Cube in a rocks glass, then add the dashes of the next four ingredients. Muddle the sugar until it has dissolved. Add the Bourbon, along with some ice, then stir. Garnish with the Twist of Lemon.

BIG MAMU

After one sip, you won't be able to speak a word of Tahitian.

INGREDIENTS:

1 jigger Gold Rhum
½ jigger Pineapple Juice
Juice of ½ Lime
3 drops Green Chartreuse
3 drops White Crème de Cacao

PREPARATION:

Fill your shaker with cracked ice. Add all the ingredients. Shake the mix vigorously for about thirty seconds. Strain over ice into a rocks glass.

BIKINI

After one sip, you'll need to wash away the night.

INGREDIENTS:

1 jigger Campari
½ jigger Dry Vermouth
¼ jigger Triple Sec
Orange Slice, for garnish

PREPARATION:

Fill your shaker with shaved ice. Add the ingredients.

Shake the mix vigorously for about thirty seconds. Strain into a chilled cocktail glass. Garnish with the Slice of Orange.

BLONDE STRANGER

After one sip, you'll stay up all night (for the first time).

INGREDIENTS:
> *1 jigger Light Rhum*
> *1 jigger Cointreau*
> *¼ jigger Cream*

PREPARATION:
> Fill your shaker with shaved ice. Add the ingredients. Shake and strain into a chilled cocktail glass.

A BLOODY MARY HISTORY LESSON

"TRYING TO REASON WITH HURRICANE SEASON" - *from A1A (1974)*

When Ernest Hemingway first introduced this cocktail to Hong Kong back in 1941, he wrote that he "did more than any other single factor (except the Japanese Army) to precipitate the Fall of that Crown Colony." Still, Hemingway was not the inventor of this drink.

That distinction falls upon a certain mixologist in Paris named Ferdinand "Pete" Petiot, who had been tending bar years earlier at place over there called Harry's New York Bar. Having had his own first encounter with vodka in 1920, Petiot the next year combined the spirit with tomato juice in a 50/50 proportion. Someone suggested that Pete ought to name his concoction after a certain waitress in a Chicago nightclub called the Bucket of Blood. So, he did that, but no one in Paris was impressed.

By 1933, Petiot was invited back to New York to tend the venerable King Cole Bar at the St. Regis Hotel. Mixing tomato juice with gin, they called the drink a Red Snapper and billed it as a cure for hangovers; however, others had taken to calling Petiot's original vodka recipe a Bloody Mary, supposedly for the bloody reign of the Tudor family's first Queen Mary against the Protestants.

"I initiated the Bloody Mary of today," Petiot later claimed in a 1964 interview with *The New Yorker* magazine. "It was really nothing but vodka and tomato juice when I took it over. I cover the bottom of the shaker with four large dashes of salt, two dashes of black pepper, two dashes of cayenne pepper, and a layer of Worcestershire sauce. I then add a dash of lemon juice and some cracked ice, put in two ounces of vodka and two ounces of thick tomato juice, shake, strain, and pour."

That, as they say, is a Bloody Mary.

Though this drink has also been made with gin or with rhum and still kept its name, that just doesn't make any sense. If you replace the original primary spirit with something else, then it's an altogether different concoction. Taking the vodka out of a Bloody Mary is like taking the cheese out of a cheeseburger; it cannot the same! And if you take out all the alcohol whatsoever, then it's called a Bloody Shame!

Bloody Mary

After one sip, you'll confess that you could use some rest.

Ingredients:
> *1 jigger Vodka*
> *1 jigger Thick Tomato Juice*
> *Dash Lemon Juice*
> *Dash Black Pepper*
> *2 dashes Salt*
> *2 dashes Cayenne Pepper*
> *3 dashes Worcestershire*
> *Lemon Slice, for garnish*

Preparation:
> Cover the bottom of your shaker with the Salt, Black Pepper, Cayenne, Worcestershire Sauce, and Lemon Juice.

Add crushed ice, along with the Vodka and the Tomato Juice. Shake the mix vigorously for about thirty seconds. Strain over ice into a collins glass. Garnish with the Slice of Lemon.

BLOODY BISHOP

Substitute Sherry for Vodka

BLOODY FAIRY

Substitute Absinthe for Vodka

BLOODY GEISHA

Substitute Saki for Vodka

BLOODY MARIA

Substitute Tequila for Vodka

BLOODY MOLLY

Substitute Irish Whiskey for Vodka

BLOODY PIRATE

Substitute Dark Rhum for Vodka

BLOODY SCOTSMAN

Substitute Scotch for Vodka

BLUE GUITAR

After one sip, you'll dream what you dream.

INGREDIENTS:
> *1 jigger Tequila*
> *1 jigger Vodka*
> *½ jigger Blue Curaçao*

PREPARATION:
> Fill your shaker with crushed ice. Add the Tequila, Vodka, and Blue Curaçao. Shake the mix vigorously for about thirty seconds. Strain into a chilled cocktail glass.

BLUE HEAVEN RENDEZVOUS

After one sip, you'll burn your candle at both ends.

INGREDIENTS:
> *1 jigger Gin*
> *½ jigger Maraschino Liqueur*
> *½ jigger Lime Juice*
> *Dash, Blue Vegetable Extract*

PREPARATION:
> Fill your shaker with ice. Add in all of the ingredients. Shake the mix vigorously for about thirty seconds. Strain over ice into a chilled cocktail glass.

BLUE SKY

After one sip, you'll move like a stratus cloud.

INGREDIENTS:
> *1 jigger Light Rhum*
> *1 jigger Blue Curaçao*
> *1 jigger Cream of Coconut*
> *2 jiggers Pineapple Juice*

PREPARATION:

Fill your blender one-quarter with crushed ice. Add in all the ingredients. Blend about a minute until smooth. Pour into chilled goblet.

A BOAT DRINK HISTORY LESSON

"BOAT DRINKS" - from VOLCANO (1979)

One February night in Boston during the 1970s, Jimmy and his friends were trying to ward off a blustery blizzard by passing time in Daisy Buchanan's, a sub-sidewalk bar then owned by Boston Bruins' hockey great, Derek Sanderson. A Back Bay establishment that's still going strong, Daisy B's remains one of those bars where everybody knows your name . . . even when it's impossible for you to remember it. Jimmy's snowy episode that ended with a "borrowed" Beantown cab inspired the song, while this particular drink provided the anti-freeze.

This recipe calls for dark rhum (Jimmy favors Haiti's Rhum Barbancourt), but a Boat Drink made with white rhum is the favorite drink among the expatriates down in Amerigo (formerly called Kinja) as noted in Herman Wouk's *Don't Stop the Carnival.*

BOAT DRINK

After one sip, you'll be ready to fly to St. Somewhere.

INGREDIENTS:
> *1 jigger Rhum Barbancourt*
> *Tonic water*
> *Juice of ½ Lime*
> *Lime Wedge, for garnish*

PREPARATION:

Fill a collins glass with ice. Add the Rhum, Lime Juice, and Tonic Water, then swizzle gently. Garnish with the Wedge of Lime.

BOB ROBERTS

After one sip, you'll be hearing Hindu in the barbecue line.

INGREDIENTS:
1 jigger Dark Rhum
½ jigger Melon Liqueur
½ jigger Cointreau
Juice of ½ Lime

PREPARATION:
Fill your shaker with ice. Add the Rhum, Melon Liquer, Cointreau, and Lime Juice. Shake the mix vigorously for about thirty seconds. Strain over ice into a sour glass.

BOGART SUIT

After one sip, you'll practice how to cuss.

INGREDIENTS:
1 jigger Light Rhum
Juice of ½ Lime
½ jigger Grand Marnier
2 dashes Maraschino Liqueur
Orange Slice, for garnish

PREPARATION:
Fill your shaker with cracked ice. Add all the ingredients. Shake the mix vigorously for about thirty seconds. Strain into a chilled cocktail glass. Garnish with the Slice of Orange.

BOSTON BLIZZARD

After one sip, you'll shoot six holes in your freezer.

INGREDIENTS:
2 jiggers Bourbon
1 jigger Cranberry Juice

1 T. Lemon Juice
2 T. Simple Syrup*
Lemon Peel, for garnish

* A recipe for preparing a Simple Syrup can be found in the Glossary.

PREPARATION:
Fill the blender one-quarter with crushed ice and add the ingredients. Blend for about a minute or until smooth. Pour into a rocks glass. Garnish with the Twist of Lemon.

BRASS MONKEY

After one sip, you'll tell everything to the monkey.

INGREDIENTS:
1 jigger Light Rhum
1 jigger Vodka
2 jiggers Orange Juice
Orange Slice, for garnish

PREPARATION:
Fill your shaker with crushed ice. Add the Rhum, Vodka, and Orange Juice. Shake vigorously for about thirty seconds. Strain over ice into a rocks glass. Garnish with the Slice of Orange.

BRAZIL

After one sip, you'll punch all your fun tickets.

INGREDIENTS:
1 jigger Sherry
1 jigger Dry Vermouth
Dash Pernod
Dash Angostura Butters
Lemon Peel, for garnish

PREPARATION:

Fill your shaker with ice. Add ingredients. Shake the mix vigorously for about thirty seconds. Strain into a chilled cocktail glass. Garnish with the Twist of Lemon.

BROWN L.A. HAZE

After one sip, your days won't seem so lonely.

INGREDIENTS:

1 jigger Sabra
1 jigger Orange Juice
Orange Slice, for garnish

PREPARATION:

Fill your shaker with crushed ice, then add the Sabra and Orange Juice. Shake the mix vigorously for about thirty seconds. Strain over ice into a cocktail glass. Garnish with the Slice of Orange.

- C -

CAFÉ DE PARIS

After one sip, you'll look for answers to bothersome questions.

INGREDIENTS:

2 jiggers Dry Gin
3 dashes Anisette
1 t. Cream
1 Egg White**

** Due to the slight risk of Salmonella or other food-borne illness, I always must recommend caution in consuming raw egg whites. To reduce this risk, always use only clean, fresh, grade A or AA eggs that have been properly refrigerated. Be certain that their shells have remained intact and avoid contact between the yolks or whites and the shell.

PREPARATION:

Fill your bar glass with ice. Add in all of the ingredients. Shake vigorously so that the cream and the egg white create a froth. Strain into a sour glass.

A Cajun Martini History Lesson

"We Are The People Our Parents Warned Us About"

- from One Particular Harbor (1983)

When the martini itself first appeared in an 1862 drink mixing guide called *The Bon-Vivant's Companion,* written by a bartender at the Occidental Hotel in San Francisco, it was called a "Martinez." There was less gin and more vermouth than in the cocktail we know today, but the drink gradually became equal proportions, and then 2 parts gin to 1 part dry vermouth just before Prohibition kicked in. By the time the Volstead Act was repealed and World War II had ended, there was very little vermouth in the recipe at all. Arguments then turned to the rightful garnish of a lemon twist or a green olive.

Meanwhile, Ian Fleming arrived on the scene in 1960 with a postwar hero named James Bond, a British spy who cared not at all for the gin, but preferred that vodka be used instead. While you might want to pause here and debate the merits of *Shaken v. Stirred,* it is more relevant that you thank 007 for having given us the vodka martini, forerunner to this next cocktail.

Today, the Cajun Martini remains a favorite in New Orleans, especially at K-Paul's Louisiana Kitchen, where it is said to have been created by Chef Paul Prudhomme and his wife, Kay. This cocktail can be made with a commercially-prepared pepper vodka, or you can prepare your own spicy spirit: vodka or gin.

To do that, put on some rubber gloves and avoid touching your eyes and face with any parts of your hands that come into contact with the peppers. Carefully wash 3 fresh cayenne peppers, 2 fresh jalapeño peppers, and 1 habeñero pepper. Gently puncture the peppers so that the alcohol will be able to flow through them and become infused with their flavors. Add the peppers to a bottle of quality vodka or gin, then refrigerate for at least 3 days. After a week, any remaining alcohol must be strained.

When you've completed preparation of the recipe, remove and discard the gloves, then wash your hands with warm, soapy water.

CAJUN MARTINI

After one sip, you'll be ready for a round of afternoon golf.

INGREDIENTS:
> *1 jigger Pepper Vodka*
> *½ jigger Dry Vermouth*

PREPARATION:
> Fill your shaker with ice. Add the two ingredients. Shake the cocktail vigorously for about thirty seconds. Strain into a chilled cocktail glass. No garnish is recommended.

CALIFORNIA LEMONADE

After one sip, you'll believe you have it all.

INGREDIENTS:
> *1 jigger Rye Whiskey*
> *Dash Grenadine*
> *Juice of 1 Lemon*
> *Juice of 1 Lime*
> *Soda Water*
> *1 T. Powdered Sugar*
> *Lemon Slice, for garnish*

PREPARATION:
> Add the Powdered Sugar to your shaker, then fill the shaker with ice. Add the Rye, the Grenadine, and the Lemon & Lime Juices. Shake the mix vigorously for about thirty seconds. Strain over ice into a rocks glass. Top off with soda water. Garnish with the Slice of Lemon.

CALIFORNIA PROBLEM

After one sip, you'll never work in dis bidniz again.

INGREDIENTS:
> *1 jigger Vodka*

2 jiggers Grapefruit Juice
2 jiggers Orange Juice
Orange Slice, for garnish

PREPARATION:
Fill your shaker with crushed ice. Add the three ingredients. Shake the mix vigorously. Strain over ice into a rocks glass. Garnish with the Slice of Orange.

CAPE CODDER

After one sip, you'll think you hear the Vineyard Sound.

INGREDIENTS:
1 jigger Vodka
3 jiggers Cranberry Juice
Lime Wedge, for garnish

PREPARATION:
Fill your shaker with ice. Add the Vodka and Cranberry Juice. Shake the mix vigorously. Strain over ice into a collins glass. Garnish with the Wedge of Lime.

CAPTAIN COOK

After one sip, you'll discover a lot on your own.

INGREDIENTS:
1 jigger Gin
½ jigger Maraschine Liqueur
1 jigger Orange Juice
Orange Slice, for garnish

PREPARATION:
Fill your shaker with ice. Add the three ingredients. Shake the mix vigorously for about thirty seconds. Strain over ice into a rocks glass. Garnish with the Slice of Orange.

CAPTAIN'S KID

After one sip, you'll climb upon your own knee.

INGREDIENTS:
1 jigger Light Rhum
1 jigger Orange Juice
Dash Lime Juice
Orange Slice, for garnish

PREPARATION:
Fill your shaker with shaved ice. Add the Rhum and Juices. Shake the mix vigorously. Strain over ice into a rocks glass. Garnish with the Slice of Orange.

CAPTAIN TONY

After one sip, you'll know a legend never dies.

INGREDIENTS:
½ jigger Vodka
½ jigger Gin
½ jigger Light Rhum
Juice of 2 Limes
1 jigger 7-Up
Lime Wedge, for garnish

PREPARATION:
Fill your bar glass with crushed ice. Add in the first four ingredients. Swizzle, then strain over ice into a collins glass. Add the 7-Up. Garnish with the Wedge of Lime.

CARMEN MIRANDA

After one sip, you won't be able to dance like that anymore.

INGREDIENTS:
1½ jiggers Dark Rhum
½ jigger Crème de Banana

Juice of ½ Lime
3 jiggers Pineapple Juice
2 dashes Orange Bitters
4 dashes Grenadine
Cherry, for garnish
Pineapple Wedge, for garnish

PREPARATION:
Fill your shaker with crushed ice. Add the first six ingredients. Shake the mix vigorously. Strain over ice into a rocks glass. Garnish with the Cherry and the Pineapple.

CAROLINE'S TREAT

After one sip, you'll go crazy.

INGREDIENTS:
2 jiggers Kahlúa
1 jigger Tequila

PREPARATION:
Fill your shaker with shaved ice. Add the Kahlúa and Tequila. Shake the mix vigorously for about thirty seconds. Strain into a chilled cocktail glass.

CARIBBEAN BREEZE

After one sip, you'll be treetop flying.

INGREDIENTS:
2 jiggers Light Rhum
½ T. Powdered Sugar
2 T. Pineapple Juice
Dash Lime Juice
Soda Water
Half-slice of Pineapple, for garnsih

PREPARATION:
Add the Powdered Sugar to your bar glass, then fill with

shaved ice. Add the Rhum and Juices. Shake the mix vigorously for about thirty seconds. Strain over ice into a rocks glass. Top off with Soda Water. Garnish with the Slice of Pineapple.

CASABLANCA

After one sip, they'll all be looking at you, kid.

INGREDIENTS:

1 jigger Light Rhum
1½ t. Triple Sec
1½ t. Cherry Liqueur
Juice of 1 Lime

PREPARATION:

Fill your shaker with crushed ice. Add the four ingredients. Shake the mix vigorously for about thirty seconds. Strain over ice into a chilled cocktail glass.

CITRUS SENSATION

After one sip, you'll welcome the revolution.

INGREDIENTS:

2 jiggers Dry Gin
Juice of ½ Orange
Juice of ½ Lime
Juice of ¼ Lemon
Soda Water
Orange Slice, for garnish

PREPARATION:

Fill your shaker with shaved ice. Add first four ingredients. Shake the mix vigorously. Strain over ice into a rocks glass. Top off with Soda. Garnish with the Slice of Orange.

CLAMDIGGER

After one sip, you'll be ready to come out of your shell.

INGREDIENTS:
> *1 jigger Vodka*
> *2 jiggers Clam Juice*
> *2 jiggers Tomato Juice*
> *Dash Tabasco*
> *Lime Slice, for garnish*

PREPARATION:
> Pour all the liquid ingredients into a collins glass and stir. Add ice. Garnish with the Slice of Lime.

CLICHÉ

After one sip, you'll say what you mean, mean what you say.

INGREDIENTS:
> *2 jiggers Tequila*
> *½ jigger Dry Vermouth*
> *Lemon Peel, for garnish*

PREPARATION:
> Fill your bar glass with crushed ice. Add ingredients. Stir and strain into a cocktail glass. Garnish with the Twist of Lemon.

COAST OF MARSEILLES

After one sip, you'll spend all of the money you saved.

INGREDIENTS:
> *½ jigger Chambord*
> *2 jiggers Sparkling Water*
> *Juice of ½ Lemon*
> *Lemon Peel, for garnish*
> *Orange Peel, for garnish*

PREPARATION:
Add ice to a wine glass. Add the three liquid ingredients and stir gently. Garnish with the Twists of Lemon and Orange.

COLD DECK

After one sip, you'll walk like you're on a slippery sloop.

INGREDIENTS:
1 jigger Brandy
½ jigger Sweet Vermouth
½ jigger Peppermint Schnapps

PREPARATION:
Fill your shaker with crushed ice. Add the ingredients. Shake the mix vigorously for about thirty seconds. Strain into a frosted cocktail glass.

COMMODORE

After one sip, you'll be giving the orders (for another round!)

INGREDIENTS:
1½ jiggers Whiskey
Juice of ½ Lime
2 dashes Orange Bitters
1 t. Simple Syrup*

* A recipe for preparing a Simple Syrup can be found in the Glossary.

PREPARATION:
Fill your shaker with ice, then add the four ingredients. Shake the mix vigorously for about thirty seconds. Strain over ice into a rocks glass.

CONCHITA

After one sip, you'll recall the lost verse of "Margaritaville."

INGREDIENTS:
1 jigger Tequila
1 jigger Grapefruit Juice
3 dashes Lemon Juice

PREPARATION:
Pour all three ingredients into a rocks glass. Stir together thoroughly. Add ice.

COOL BREEZE

After one sip, you'll see the lightweights blown away.

INGREDIENTS:
1 jigger Vodka
2 jiggers Unsweetened Pineapple Juice
2 jiggers Cranberry Juice
1 jigger Ginger Ale

PREPARATION:
Pour the first three ingredients into a collins glass. Stir together thoroughly. Add ice Top off with Ginger Ale.

CORAL REEFER

After one sip, you won't ever start a band.

INGREDIENTS:
1 jigger Rhum
Juice of ½ Lemon
1 jigger Simple Syrup*
4 dashes Grenadine
Lemon Peel, for garnish

* A recipe for preparing a Simple Syrup can be found in the Glossary.

PREPARATION:
Fill your blender one-quarter with ice. Add the four ingredients. Blend low for about thirty seconds or until smooth. Pour into a rocks glass. Garnish with the Twist of Lemon.

CORDOBA

After one sip, you won't remember where you put the keys.

INGREDIENTS:
1 jigger Galliano
1 jigger White Crème de Cacao
2 jiggers Cream

PREPARATION:
Fill your blender one-quarter with ice. Add in all the ingredients. Blend on high speed for about thirty seconds, then strain into a frosted rocks glass.

COSMIC SHIPWRECK

After one sip, you'll finally find some need to focus.

INGREDIENTS:
1 jigger Gin
¼ jigger Fresh Lime Juice
1 t. Fine Granulated Sugar
6 dashes Bitters
Lime Slice, for garnish

PREPARATION:
Add the sugar to your bar glass, then top with shaved ice. Add the remaining ingredients. Shake vigorously until frost forms on the outside of the shaker. Strain over cracked ice into a collins glass. Garnish with the Slice of Lime.

Costa del Sol

After one sip, you'll be glad that life's a beach.

INGREDIENTS:
2 jiggers Gin
1 jigger Grand Marnier
1 jigger Apricot Brandy
Orange Slice, for garnish

PREPARATION:
Fill your shaker with crushed ice. Add in the liquid ingredients. Shake the mix vigorously for about thirty seconds. Strain over ice into a rocks glass. Garnish with the Slice of Orange.

Cousin in Miami

After one sip, you'll understand the impromptu.

INGREDIENTS:
1 jigger Rhum
¼ jigger Triple Sec
Dash Orange Juice
Orange Slice, for garnish

PREPARATION:
Fill your shaker with crushed ice. Add the ingredients. Shake the mix vigorously. Strain over ice into a rocks glass. Garnish with the Slice of Orange.

Cousin in Miami Beach

After one sip, you'll get that old panache.

INGREDIENTS:
1 jigger Light Rhum
½ jigger White Crème de Menthe
Dash Lime Juice

PREPARATION:
Fill your shaker with shaved ice. Add all three ingredients. Shake the mix vigorously for about thirty seconds. Strain over ice into a rocks glass.

COWBOY IN THE JUNGLE

After one sip, you'll roll with the punches.

INGREDIENTS:
1 jigger Light Rhum
½ jigger Frangelico
Juice of 1 Lime
1 t. Grenadine
Lime Slice, for garnish

PREPARATION:
Fill your shaker with crushed ice. Add the ingredients. Shake the mix vigorously for about thirty seconds. Strain over ice into a rocks glass. Garnish with the Slice of Lime.

CREOLA

After one sip, you'll repeat words a thousand times a day.

INGREDIENTS:
1 jigger Extra Dry Vermouth
1 jigger Sweet Vermouth
2 dashes Benedictine
2 dashes Bitters
Lemon Peel, for garnish

PREPARATION:
Fill your bar glass with ice. Add the ingredients. Stir the mix thoroughly, then strain into a chilled cocktail glass. Garnish with the Twist of Lemon.

CUBA LIBRE

After one sip, you'll think it's 90 miles to freedom.

INGREDIENTS:
> *1 jigger Light Havana Club Rhum*
> *½ jigger Dark Havana Club Rhum*
> *½ jigger Coca Cola*
> *½ t. Sugar*
> *Juice of 1 Lime*
> *Lime Peel, for garnish*

PREPARATION:
> Place three ice cubes in a collins glass. Add the liquid ingredients and stir thoroughly. Garnish with the Twist of Lime.

CUBAN CRIME OF PASSION

After one sip, you'll feel messy and old fashioned.

INGREDIENTS:
> *1½ jiggers Havana Club Rhum*
> *½ jigger Passion-Fruit Nectar*
> *1 jigger Lime Juice*
> *Lime Slice, for garnish*

PREPARATION:
> Fill your shaker with shaved ice. Add all three ingredients. Shake the mix vigorously for about thirty seconds. Strain over ice into a rocks glass. Garnish with the Slice of Lime.

CUGAT

After one sip, you'll do the rhumba as no one else dares.

INGREDIENTS:
> *1 jigger Dry Gin*
> *1 jigger Dry Vermouth*

4 dashes Kümmel
4 dashes Charbreux
2 dashes Pineapple Syrup
Lime Peel, for garnish

PREPARATION:

Fill your shaker with ice. Add the liquid ingredients. Shake the mix vigorously for about thirty seconds. Strain over ice into a rocks glass. Garnish with the Twist of Lime.

- D -

A Daiquirí History Lesson

"The Weather is Here, I Wish You Were Beautiful"

- from *Coconut Telegraph* (1981)

Sometimes spelled with a capital letter, this fruity concoction is named after a Cuban town not far from Santiago, where Americans ventured to work the mines after the Spanish-American War in 1898. Spending long days laboring beneath the ground, the Yanks would relax each weekend at the Hotel Venus, where they would slug these rhum drinks down. The Daiquirí had been given its name by Jennings S. Cox, chief engineer of the mining project, and many even credit him with its creation.

A generation would pass, though, before any printed reference to such a drink first appeared in 1920, when F. Scott Fitzgerald mentioned it in *This Side of Paradise*.

Meanwhile, you will notice that there is not a great deal of distinction among the Daiquirí, the Mojito, and the Papa Dobles, all of which called for a mix of rhum and lime juice and were the favorites of Papa Hemingway. Then, again, what drink was not a favorite of the old boy?

DAIQUIRÍ (BASIC)

After one sip, you won't surface for a week . . . maybe two!

INGREDIENTS:
1 jigger Light Rhum
½ jigger Lime Juice
1 t. Superfine Sugar
Lime Slice, for garnish

PREPARATION:
Add the sugar to a bar glass, then the Lime Juice and the Rhum. Fill the glass with ice, then shake it for about thirty seconds. Strain over ice into a sour glass. Garnish with the Slice of Lime.

DAIQUIRÍ (FROZEN)

As with the Basic Daiquirí, this frozen concoction also has some literary connections, for it was first blended at La Florida Bar in Havana, a place affectionately known as "Floridita" when Hemingway still occupied a seat.

INGREDIENTS:
1 jigger Light Rhum
½ jigger Lime Juice
1 t. Superfine Sugar
Lime Slice, for garnish

PREPARATION:
Add the sugar to the blender, then fill one-quarter with ice. Add the Lime Juice and Rhum. Blend low until smooth. Pour into a rocks glass. Garnish with the Slice of Lime.

FROZEN FRUIT DAIQUIRÍ

If you're going this route, then make certain that your choice of fruit matches your choice of liqueur. For example, if you are making a Black Raspberry Daiquirí, be certain to use Chambord as the liqueur. If your fruit is not sweet, you may add ½ jigger of honey.

INGREDIENTS:
> 1 jigger Light Rhum
> ½ jigger Lime Juice
> ½ jigger Fruit Liqueur
> 1 jigger Cream
> ¼ cup of the Fruit
> Selected piece of Fruit, for garnish

PREPARATION:
> Fill your blender one-quarter with ice. Add in all of the ingredients. Blend low until smooth. Pour into a chilled rocks glass. Garnish with the selected piece of Fruit.

DAMN THE WEATHER

After one sip, you'll be drinking barometer soup.

INGREDIENTS:
> 1 jigger Gin
> ¼ jigger Triple Sec
> ½ jigger Sweet Vermouth
> ½ jigger Orange Juice

PREPARATION:
> Fill your bar glass with crushed ice. Add the ingredients. Shake vigorously until a condensation appears on the outside of the glass. Strain into a chilled cocktail glass.

DARK & STORMY

The drink of choice for sailors off Bermuda is this classic cocktail made with the island's Black Seal Rum and ginger beer. Before Americans ever thought of inventing the milder ginger ale, ginger beer was the stronger soft drink made from the distinctive essence of that flavorful root. And while there are several commercial brands of ginger beer on the market other than Stewart's, be sure to read the ingredients on their labels so that you do not use one made with any sort of fruit juice as its base. Pineapple juice is not only common, but also quite disgusting. [In the event that you cannot find a good, commercial ginger beer, there is a recipe in the Glossary.]

Your Dark & Stormy should warm your mouth with a subtle burn of dark rum and ginger, further enhanced with the lime.

INGREDIENTS:
>1 jigger Gosling's Black Seal Rum
>Stewart's Ginger Beer
>Lime Wedge, for garnish

PREPARATION:
Fill a rocks glass with ice. Add the Black Seal Rum, then top off with the Ginger Beer. Stir gently. Garnish with the Wedge of Lime.

DECKHAND

After one sip, others will find it difficult to follow in your wake.

INGREDIENTS:
>1½ jiggers Whiskey
>1 jigger Sweet Vermouth
>1 dash Jamaican Ginger, grated fresh

PREPARATION:
Fill your bar glass with ice. Add the ingredients. Stir and strain over ice into a chilled cocktail glass.

DEPTH CHARGE

After one sip, you'll be down to rock bottom again.

INGREDIENTS:
>1 jigger Dry Gin
>1 jigger Lillet

2 dashes Pernod
Orange Peel, for garnish

PREPARATION:
Fill your shaker with ice. Add the Gin, Lillet, and Pernod. Shake for about thirty seconds and strain into a chilled cocktail glass. Garnish with the Twist of Orange.

DESDEMONA

After one sip, you'll have a passion for more than just cookies.

INGREDIENTS:
1 jigger Light Rhum
Juice of ½ Lemon
4 dashes Grenadine
2 jiggers Tonic Water
Lemon Wedge, for garnish

PREPARATION:
Fill a rocks glass with ice. Add the ingredients and swizzle gently. Garnish with the Wedge of Lemon.

DESDEMONA'S ROCKET SHIP

After one sip, you'll have a blast.

INGREDIENTS:
1 jigger Rhum
½ jigger Dry Vermouth
½ jigger Swedish Punsch
Dash Grenadine

PREPARATION:
Fill your shaker with cracked ice. Add together all the ingredients. Shake and strain into a chilled cocktail glass.

DIAMOND AS BIG AS THE RITZ

After one sip, you'll know this is not an everyday temptation.

INGREDIENTS:
1 jigger Gin
Juice of 1 Lemon
1 t. Powdered Sugar
Champagne
Lemon Peel, for garnish

PREPARATION:
Add the Sugar to the bottom of a bar glass. Fill the glass with crushed ice. Add the Gin and the Lemon Juice. Shake the mix vigorously. Strain into a chilled cocktail glass. Top with Champagne. Garnish with the Twist of Lemon.

DIVINE ANDREW

After one sip, you'll struggle to picture your own autograph.

INGREDIENTS:
1 jigger Dry Gin
1 jigger Dry Sherry
1 jigger Dubonnet
2 dashes Orange Bitters
Lemon Peel, for garnish

PREPARATION:
Fill your bar glass with ice. Add the Gin, Sherry, Dubonnet, and Bitters. Stir thoroughly. Strain into a chilled cocktail glass. Garnish with the Twist of Lemon.

DIXIE

After one sip, your mouth will feel like cotton.

INGREDIENTS:
1 jigger Gin

½ *jigger Abisante*
½ *jigger Dry Vermouth*
Juice of ¼ Orange
2 dashes Grenadine
Orange Peel, for garnish

PREPARATION:
Fill your shaker with ice. Add in all of the ingredients. Shake and strain into a chilled cocktail glass. Garnish with the Twist of Orange.

DOMINICAN COOLER

After one sip, you'll fly to Haiti without any plane.

INGREDIENTS:
1 jigger Light Rhum
½ *jigger Amaretto*
½ *jigger Pineapple Juice*
½ *jigger Coconut Cream*
1 t. Grenadine
½ *jigger Milk*
Pineapple Wedge, for garnish

PREPARATION:
Fill your blender one-quarter with crushed ice. Add in the liquid ingredients. Blend until smooth. Strain into a chilled goblet. Garnish with the Wedge of Pineapple.

DOMINO COLLEGE GRAD

After one sip, you know you're gonna fall on your face.

INGREDIENTS:
1 jigger Dark Rhum
½ *jigger Cointreau*
½ *jigger Lime Juice*

PREPARATION:

Fill your shaker with ice. Add the ingredients. Shake and strain over ice into a chilled glass.

DOOR NUMBER THREE

After one sip, you'll be ready to make any deal.

INGREDIENTS:

1 jigger Dry Gin
Dash Grenadine
Dash Apricot Brandy
Juice of ½ Lime
Lime Peel, for garnish

PREPARATION:

Fill your shaker with ice. Add all four ingredients. Shake the mix vigorously for about thirty seconds. Strain into a chilled cocktail glass. Garnish with the Twist of Lime.

DOWN THE HATCH

After one sip, you'll be decked.

INGREDIENTS:

1 jigger Whiskey
3 dashes Blackberry Brandy
2 dashes Orange Bitters
Orange Peel, for garnish

PREPARATION:

Fill your shaker with ice. Add the ingredients. Shake the mix vigorously for about thirty seconds. Strain over ice into a chilled cocktail glass. Garnish with the Twist of Orange.

DREAMSICLE

After one sip, you'll have to guess your own occupation.

INGREDIENTS:
> *1 jigger Galliano*
> *1 jigger White Crème de Cacao*
> *1½ jiggers Cream*
> *2 jiggers Orange Juice*
> *Orange Slice, for garnish*

PREPARATION:
> Fill your shaker with ice. Add all four ingredients. Shake the mix vigorously for about thirty seconds. Strain over ice into a rocks glass. Garnish with the Slice of Orange.

DUKE'S SUNDAE

After one sip, you'll be feelin' good and feelin' right,.

INGREDIENTS:
> *1 jigger Leilani Rhum*
> *½ jigger Cointreau*
> *½ jigger Pineapple Juice*
> *½ t. Grenadine*
> *Pineapple Spear, for garnish*

PREPARATION:
> Fill your shaker with ice. Add the liquid ingredients. Shake the mix vigorously for about thirty seconds. Strain into a chilled cocktail glass. Garnish with the Spear of Pineapple.

- E -

EARTHQUAKE

After one sip, you'll start to shake, rattle, and roll.

INGREDIENTS:
1 jigger American Whiskey
1 jigger Gin
1 jigger Anesone or Abisante
Lemon Slice, for garnish

PREPARATION:
Fill your shaker with ice. Add all three ingredients. Shake the mix vigorously for about thirty seconds. Strain over ice into a rocks glass. Garnish with the Slice of Lemon.

ECLIPSE

After one sip, you'll overshadow yourself.

INGREDIENTS:
1 jigger Sloe Gin
½ jigger Gin
3 dashes Grenadine
Maraschino Cherry, for garnish

PREPARATION:
Drop the Cherry into a rocks glass. Cover with Grenadine. Fill your shaker with crushed ice. Add the 2 Gins. Shake

and carefully strain the gin mixture over the back of a spoon so that it floats atop the Grenadine.

EL DIABLO

After one sip, you'll start to raise hell.

INGREDIENTS:
> *1 jigger Tequila*
> *½ jigger Crème de Cassis*
> *Juice of ½ Lime*
> *Ginger Ale*
> *Lime Slice, for garnish*

PREPARATION:
> Fill a collins glass with ice. Add the Tequila, the Crème de Cassis, and the Juice. Stir. Add the Ginger Ale and swizzle gently. Garnish with the Slice of Lime.

ELVIS IMPERSONATOR

After one sip, you just might become the next best thing.

INGREDIENTS:
> *1 jigger Tennessee Whiskey*
> *1 jigger Gin*
> *Juice of ½ Lemon*
> *Juice of ½ Orange*
> *1 Egg White***
> *1 t. Apricot Brandy*
> *½ t. Powdered Sugar*

> *** Due to the slight risk of Salmonella or other food-borne illness, I always must recommend caution in consuming raw egg whites. To reduce this risk, always use only clean, fresh, grade A or AA eggs that have been properly refrigerated. Be certain that their shells have remained intact and avoid contact between the yolks or whites and the shell.*

PREPARATION:

Place the sugar in the bottom of a bar glass, then stir in the Brandy and Juices to dissolve the sugar. Fill the bar glass with ice, and add the Tennessee Whiskey, Gin, and Egg White. Shake the mix vigorously for about thirty seconds and strain into a sour glass.

EVERLASTING MOONIE

After one sip, you'll have the perfect alibi.

INGREDIENTS:
1 jigger Gold Tequila
1 jigger Kahlúa

PREPARATION:
Pour the two ingredients over ice in a rocks glass.

EVE'S CAT

After one sip, you'll be tempted to know everyone else.

INGREDIENTS:
½ t. Pernod
1 T. Cognac
2 t. Curaçao
2 t. Sugar
Pink Sparkling Wine
Orange Peel, for garnish

PREPARATION:
Measure the Cognac and the Curaçao in a bar glass. Add the Sugar and allow it to dissolve. Meanwhile, add the Pernod to a large wine glass and swirl to coat the inside. Stir together the ingredients of the bar glass, then pour them into the large wine glass. Stir again. Add ice. Top with the Pink Sparkling Wine. Garnish with the Twist of Orange.

EVERGLADE

After one sip, you'll act like an environmental terrorist.

INGREDIENTS:
>*1 jigger Light Rhum*
>*1 jigger White Crème de Cacao*
>*1 jigger Cream*
>*½ jigger Kahlúa*
>*Orange Slice, for garnish*

PREPARATION:
>Fill your shaker with crushed ice. Add in all the ingredients. Shake the mix vigorously for about thirty seconds and strain over ice into a rocks glass. Garnish with the Slice of Orange.

EVERYONE'S BWANA

After one sip, you'll want to learn how to score.

INGREDIENTS:
>*1 jigger Vodka*
>*1 jigger Banana Liqueur*
>*1 jigger Cream*

PREPARATION:
>Fill your shaker with shaved ice. Add the the Vodka, Banana Liqueur, and the Cream. Shake the mix vigorously for about thirty seconds. Strain over ice into a rocks glass.

EXPATRIATED AMERICAN

After one sip, you'll be hoping to have some fun.

INGREDIENTS:
>*2 jiggers Spiced Rhum*
>*3 jiggers Grapefruit Juice*

½ t. *Powdered Sugar*
Dash Grated Cinnamon
Dash Grated Nutmeg

PREPARATION:

Fill a bar glass with cracked ice, then add the Spiced
Rhum and Grapefruit Juice. Stir them together thoroughly
and strain over ice into a rocks glass. Dust with the Powdered Sugar, Cinnamon, and Nutmeg.

- F -

FAIR AND WARMER

After one sip, you'll know the weather is here.

INGREDIENTS:
2 jiggers Light Rhum
1 jigger Sweet Vermouth
2 dashes Curaçao
Lemon Peel, for garnish

PREPARATION:
Fill your shaker with ice. Add the Rhum, Sweet Vermouth, and Curaçao. Stir them together and strain over ice into a rocks glass. Garnish with the Twist of Lemon.

FAUSTO'S CHOCOLATE MILK

After one sip, your head will hurt and your feet will stink.

INGREDIENTS:
1½ jiggers Chocolate Vodka
1½ jiggers Crème de Cacao
1 jigger Bailey's Irish Cream
2 jiggers Cream

PREPARATION:
Fill your blender one-quarter with cracked ice. Add the

Vodka, Crème de Cacao, Bailey's, and Cream. Blend until smooth and frothy. Pour into a frosted goblet.

FESTIVAL

After one sip, you'll be ready to start the Carnival.

INGREDIENTS:
> ½ jigger Crème de Cacao
> 1 T. Apricot Brandy
> 1 t. Grenadine
> ½ jigger Cream

PREPARATION:
> Fill your shaker with crushed ice. Add all four ingredients. Shake the mix vigorously for at least thirty seconds. Strain over ice into a rocks glass.

FIJI FIZZ

After one sip, you'll behave like the Big Mamu.

INGREDIENTS:
> 1 jigger Dark Rhum
> ½ jigger Bourbon
> 1 t. Cherry Brandy
> 3 dashes Orange Bitters
> 2 jiggers Cola
> Orange Slice, for garnish

PREPARATION:
> Fill your shaker with crushed ice. Add in the first four ingredients. Shake the mix vigorously for about thirty seconds, then strain over ice into a collins glass. Add the Cola. Swizzle gently, once or twice. Garnish with the Slice of Orange.

FINGERS

After one sip, you'll feel in harmonic concordance.

INGREDIENTS:
1 jigger Dark Rhum
Juice of ½ Lemon
2 dashes Grenadine
¼ t. Grated Nutmeg

PREPARATION:
Fill your shaker with ice. Add the Rhum, Lemon Juice, and Grenadine. Shake the mix vigorously for about thirty seconds. Strain over ice into a cocktail glass. Dust with the Grated Nutmeg.

FINS

After one sip, you'll feel like a remora.

INGREDIENTS:
1 jigger Dark Rhum
Orange juice
2 dashes Grenadine
Orange Slice, for garnish

PREPARATION:
Fill your shaker with ice. Add the Rhum, Orange Juice, and Grenadine. Shake (first, to the left; then, to right). Strain into chilled cocktail glass. Garnish with the Slice of Orange.

FISH OUT OF WATER

After one sip, you'll be hooked, line and sinker.

INGREDIENTS:
1 jigger Light Rhum
½ jigger Triple Sec
Juice of ½ Lemon

Juice of ½ Orange
Orange Peel, for garnish

PREPARATION:
Fill your shaker with crushed ice. Add the Rhum, Triple Sec, and both Juices. Shake the mix vigorously for about thirty seconds. Strain into a chilled cocktail glass. Garnish with the Twist of Orange.

FLAMINGO (STANDING ON LEFT LEG)

After one sip, you'll try to lift both legs.

INGREDIENTS:
1 jigger Apricot Brandy
Juice of 1 Lime
3 jiggers Gin
2 dashes Grenadine
Lime Peel, for garnish

PREPARATION:
Fill your shaker with cracked ice. Add all four ingredients. Shake the mix vigorously. Strain into a chilled cocktail glass. Garnish with the Twist of Lime.

FLAMINGO (STANDING ON RIGHT LEG)

After one sip, you'll be put out on the front lawn.

INGREDIENTS:
1 jigger Dark Rhum
1 jigger Pineapple Juice
Juice of 1 Lime
½ jigger Grenadine
Lime Peel, for garnish

PREPARATION:
Fill your shaker with crushed ice. Add the Rhum, Juices, and Grenadine. Shake the mix vigorously for about thirty

seconds. Strain into a chilled cocktail glass. Garnish with the Twist of Lime.

FLAUBERT

After one sip, you'll really love the library.

INGREDIENTS:
1 jigger Light Rhum
1 T. Passion Fruit Syrup
1 T. Lime Juice
Lime Peel, for garnish

PREPARATION:
Fill your blender one-quarter with cracked ice. Add the Rhum, Passion Fruit Syrup, and Lime Juice. Blend about thirty seconds until smooth. Pour into a chilled cocktail glass. Garnish with the Twist of Lime.

FLIRTING WITH THE MERMAID

After one sip, you might become the catch of the day.

INGREDIENTS:
1 jigger Light Rhum
½ jigger Cherry Brandy
2 jiggers Orange Juice
2 dashes Orange Bitters
Orange Slice, for garnish

PREPARATION:
Fill a collins glass with ice. Add the Rhum, Brandy, Orange Juice, and Bitters. Stir thoroughly. Garnish with the Slice of Orange.

FLORIDA PUNCH

After one sip, you'll be at the corner of Walk/Don't Walk.

INGREDIENTS:
> *1 jigger Dark Rhum*
> *½ jigger Brandy*
> *½ jigger Grapefruit Juice*
> *½ jigger Orange Juice*
> *Orange Slice, for garnish*

PREPARATION:
> Fill your shaker with shaved ice. Add all four ingredients. Shake the mix vigorously until a condensation appears on the outside of the shaker. Strain over ice into a rocks glass. Garnish with the Slice of Orange.

FLORIDAY

After one sip, you'll be hopin' for the give without the take.

INGREDIENTS:
> *1¼ jiggers Light Rhum*
> *1 t. Dry Vermouth*
> *1 t. Sweet Vermouth*
> *1 jigger Grapefruit Juice*
> *Lemon Peel, for garnish*

PREPARATION:
> Fill your shaker with shaved ice. Add all four ingredients. Shake the mix vigorously. Strain into a chilled cocktail glass. Garnish with the Twist of Lemon.

FLYING DUTCHMAN

After one sip, you'll behave like some Remittance Man.

INGREDIENTS:
> *1 jigger Gin*

½ *jigger Triple Sec*
Orange Peel, for garnish

PREPARATION:
Add ice to a rocks glass. Add the Gin and Triple Sec, then stir. Garnish with the Twist of Orange.

FOG CUTTER

After one sip, you'll feel alone on a midnight passage.

INGREDIENTS:
1½ jiggers Light Rhum
½ jigger Brandy
½ jigger Gin
1 jigger Orange Juice
1 jigger Lemon Juice
½ jigger Orgeat Syrup
1 t. Sherry

PREPARATION:
Fill your shaker with cracked ice. Add all of the ingredients *except* for the Sherry. Shake the mix vigorously, then strain over ice into a collins glass. Float the Sherry on top.

FOGGY DAY

After one sip, you won't know which direction to head.

INGREDIENTS:
1 jigger Gin
½ jigger Pernod
Lemon Peel, for garnish

PREPARATION:
Fill your shaker with ice. Add the Gin and Pernod, then shake the mix for about thirty seconds. Strain into over ice into a cocktail glass. Garnish with the Twist of Lemon.

FOG HORN

After one sip, you'll be ready to let off some steam.

INGREDIENTS:
2 jiggers Gin
Ginger Ale
Lemon Slice, for garnish

PREPARATION:
Fill a collins glass with ice. Add the Gin and Ginger Ale, then swizzle lightly. Garnish with the Slice of Lemon.

FOLLOW THE EQUATOR

After one sip, you'll attempt to meet the Twain.

INGREDIENTS:
1 jigger Gin
1 jigger Green Crème de Menthe
1 jigger Pineapple juice

PREPARATION:
Fill your shaker with shaved ice. Add all three ingredients. Shake the mixture and strain over ice into a rocks glass.

FOXY LADY

After one sip, you'll try to order a double Bar Mitzvah.

INGREDIENTS:
1 jigger Amaretto
1 jigger Dark Crème de Cacao
2 jiggers Cream

PREPARATION:
Fill your shaker with shaved ice. Add the three ingredients. Shake the mix vigorously and strain over ice into a rocks glass.

FRENCHMAN FOR THE NIGHT

After one sip, you'll blame everything on Monet.

INGREDIENTS:
> *1 jigger Gin*
> *1 jigger Dry Vermouth*
> *1 jigger Crème de Cassis*
> *Cherry, for garnish*

PREPARATION:
> Fill your shaker with cracked ice. Add together the liquid ingredients. Shake them vigorously, then strain into a chilled cocktail glass. Garnish with the Cherry.

FRENZY

After one sip, you'll feel real palsy-walsy.

INGREDIENTS:
> *1 jigger Light Rhum*
> *½ t. Powdered Sugar*
> *Juice of 1 Lime*
> *½ oz. Grenadine*
> *Lime Slice, for garnish*

PREPARATION:
> Spoon the Sugar into the bottom of your bar glass, then fill with ice. Add the Rhum, Juice, and Grenadine. Shake together, then strain over ice into a sour glass. Garnish with the Slice of Lime.

- G -

GALE AT SEA

After one sip, you'll think it's Windsday.

INGREDIENTS:
1 jigger Vodka
½ jigger Dry Vermouth
½ jigger Galliano
½ jigger Blue Curaçao
Orange Peel, for garnish

PREPARATION:
Fill your shaker with crushed ice. Add the Vodka, Dry Vermouth, Galliano, and Blue Curaçao. Shake them together thoroughly, then strain into a chilled cocktail glass. Garnish with the Twist of Orange.

GECKO

After one sip, you'll be off to see the lizard.

1 jigger Tequila
½ jigger Kahlúa
½ jigger White Crème de Cacao
2 dashes Curaçao
Orange Peel, for garnish

PREPARATION:

Fill your shaker with ice. Add all the ingredients. Shake the mix vigorously for about thirty seconds. Strain over ice into a cocktail glass. Garnish with the Twist of Orange.

GEORGIA PEACH FIZZ

After one sip, you won't even know what's on your mind.

INGREDIENTS:

1 jigger Brandy
½ jigger Peach Brandy
½ jigger Lemon Juice
1 t. Banana Liqueur
1 t. Simple Syrup*
Club Soda
Peach Slice, for garnish

* A recipe for preparing a Simple Syrup can be found in the Glossary.

PREPARATION:

Fill your shaker with ice. Add the Brandies, Lemon Juice, Banana Liqueur, and Simple Syrup. Shake the mixture vigorously, then strain over ice into a collins glass. Top off with Soda. Garnish with the Slice of Peach.

GOD'S OWN DRINK

After one sip, you'll think it's purer than bottled holy water.

INGREDIENTS:

1 jigger Vodka
½ jigger Clam Juice
½ jigger Beef Bouillon
Dash Heinz 57
Dash Tabasco
Lemon Wedge, for garnish

PREPARATION:

Fill your shaker with crushed ice. Add in the first five ingredients. Shake the mix vigorously. Strain over ice into a collins glass. Garnish with the Wedge of Lemon.

GODZILLA'S BREATH

After one sip, you'll be vaporizing cars.

INGREDIENTS:

> 1 jigger Jamaican Rhum
> 1 jigger Apricot Brandy
> 1 jigger Sloe Gin
> Juice of 1 Lime
> Dash Grenadine
> Lime Wedge, for garnish

PREPARATION:

Fill your shaker with ice. Add the liquid ingredients. Shake them together thoroughly, then strain over ice into a rocks glass. Garnish with the Wedge of Lime.

GONG SHOW

After one sip, you'll want to wear a paper bag over your head.

INGREDIENTS:

> 1 jigger Vodka
> ½ jigger White Crème de Cacao
> 1 jigger Lemon Juice
> Dash Grenadine
> Lemon Peel, for garnish

PREPARATION:

Fill your shaker with ice. Add the Vodka, Crème de Cacao, Juice, and Grenadine. Shake together and strain into a chilled cocktail glass. Garnish with the Twist of Lemon.

GRAPEFRUIT HIGHBALL

After one sip, you'll become thick-skinned, but yellow.

INGREDIENTS:
> *1 jigger Light Rhum*
> *Juice of 2 Grapefruit*

PREPARATION:
> Add ice to highball glass. Add the Rhum and Grapefruit Juice. Stir a time or two. Bottoms up!

GRAPEFRUIT/JUICY FRUIT

After one sip, you'll commit a little mortal sin.

INGREDIENTS:
> *1 jigger Midori*
> *1 jigger Crème de Banana*
> *1 jigger Orange Juice*
> *1 jigger Grapefruit Juice*
> *½ jigger Grenadine*

PREPARATION:
> Fill your shaker with ice. Add together the ingredients. Shake and strain over ice into a collins glass.

GRAVITY STORM

After one sip, you'll realize that you're earthly bound.

INGREDIENTS:
> *1 jigger Light Rhum*
> *½ jigger Sweet Vermouth*
> *1 t. Applejack*
> *1 t. Lemon Juice*
> *2 dashes Grenadine*
> *Lemon Peel, for garnish*

PREPARATION:

Fill your shaker with ice. Add the Rhum, Vermouth, Applejack, Lemon Juice, and Grenadine. Shake the mix vigorously for about thirty seconds. Strain into a chilled cocktail glass. Garnish with the Twist of Lemon.

GREEN LIZARD

After one sip, you'll sing: "I'm tired and Iguana go to bed."

INGREDIENTS:

1 jigger Green Chartreuse
½ jigger 151 Proof Rhum
Lime Peel, for garnish

PREPARATION:

Fill your shaker with shaved ice. Add the Green Chartreuse and Rhum. Shake the mixture together thoroughly, then strain over ice into a rocks glass. Garnish with the Twist of Lime.

GULFSTREAM SQUALL

After one sip, you'll sleep 'til way past noon.

INGREDIENTS:

1 jigger Grand Marnier
1 jigger Dry Gin
½ jigger Lemon Juice
½ jigger Lime Juice
Orange Peel, for garnish

PREPARATION:

Fill your shaker with crushed ice. Add the Grand Marnier, Gin, and Juices. Shake the mix vigorously for about thirty seconds. Strain over ice into a rocks glass. Garnish with the Twist of Orange.

GUMBO FIZZ

After one sip, you'll be speaking mumbo-jumbo.

INGREDIENTS:

1 jigger Gin
Juice of ½ Lemon
1 t. Superfine Sugar
1 Egg White**
1 t. Cointreau
½ jigger Cream
2 jiggers Club Soda
Lemon Slice, for garnish

** Due to the slight risk of Salmonella or other food-borne illness, I always must recommend caution in consuming raw egg whites. To reduce this risk, always use only clean, fresh, grade A or AA eggs that have been properly refrigerated. Be certain that their shells have remained intact and avoid contact between the yolks or whites and the shell.

PREPARATION:

Spoon the Sugar into the bottom of your bar glass, then fill the glass with ice. Add the Egg White, then the Gin, Lemon Juice, Cointreau, and Cream. Shake the mixture vigorously until the Egg White begins to froth. Strain over ice into a collins glass. Add Club Soda, then stir gently. Garnish with the Slice of Lemon.

GYPSY IN THE PALACE

After one sip, you'll say there ain't no wrong or right.

INGREDIENTS:

1 jigger Vodka
½ jigger Benedictine
1 t. Lemon Juice
1 t. Orange Juice
Orange Slice, for garnish

PREPARATION:

Fill your shaker with shaved ice. Add the Vodka,
Benedictine, and the Juices. Shake them together and
strain over ice into a rocks glass. Garnish with the Slice
of Orange.

- H -

HAVANA CLUB

After one sip, you might try what the people like to read about up in America.

INGREDIENTS:
> *1 jigger Havana Club Rhum*
> *1 jigger Dry Vermouth*
> *Lemon Peel, for garnish*

PREPARATION:
> Fill your shaker with ice. Add the two ingredients. Shake the mix vigorously, then strain it over ice into a chilled cocktail glass. Garnish with the Twist of Lemon.

HAVANA DAYDREAM

After one sip, you'll be looking for some mystery man.

INGREDIENTS:
> *1 jigger Havana Club Rhum*
> *½ jigger White Crème de Cacao*
> *1 t. Green Chartreuse*
> *1 jigger Pineapple Juice*
> *Juice of ½ Lime*
> *Lime Peel, for garnish*

PREPARATION:

Fill your shaker with ice. Add the Rhum, White Crème de Cacao, Green Chartreuse, and Juices. Shake the mix vigorously for about thirty seconds. Strain over ice into a rocks glass. Garnish with the Twist of Lime.

HAVANA STANDARD

After one sip, you'll be thinking about the money you made.

INGREDIENTS:

1 jigger Havana Club Rhum
¾ jigger Pineapple Juice
¼ jigger Lemon Juice
Lemon Slice, for garnish

PREPARATION:

Fill your shaker with ice. Add the Rhum and Juices. Shake them together, then strain into a chilled cocktail glass. Garnish with the Slice of Lemon.

HEMISPHERE DANCER

After one sip, you'll be hiding your secrets like contraband.

INGREDIENTS:

1 jigger Brandy
½ jigger Cointreau
1 t. Anisette
Orange Peel, for garnish

PREPARATION:

Fill your shaker with ice. Add together the Brandy, Cointreau, and Anisette. Shake the mix vigorously. Strain into a chilled cocktail glass. Garnish with the Twist of Orange.

HIGH JAMAICAN WIND

After one sip, your head will be turning around.

INGREDIENTS:

1 jigger Dark Jamaican Rhum
½ jigger Kahlúa
½ jigger Cream

PREPARATION:

Add ice to a rocks glass. Pour in the Kahlúa and Cream, then stir. Gently pour the Dark Jamaican Rhum over the back of a spoon so that the Rhum floats atop the other ingredients.

HIGH TIDE

After one sip, you'll be in over your head.

INGREDIENTS:

½ jigger Bourbon
1 jigger Dry Vermouth
¼ jigger Lemon Juice
Lemon Peel, for garnish

PREPARATION:

Fill your shaker with ice. Add the Bourbon, Vermouth and Juice. Shake the mix vigorously, the strain over ice into a chilled cocktail glass. Garnish with the Twist of Lemon.

HOLY GHOST

After one sip, you'll talk denial and dysfunctional things.

INGREDIENTS:

1 jigger St. Raphaël
½ jigger Gin
Orange Peel, for garnish

PREPARATION:
Fill your bar glass with ice. Add the St. Raphaël and Gin. Stir gently fot only a few seconds, then strain into a chilled cocktail glass. Garnish with the Twist of Orange.

HONEY DO

After one sip, you'll want to do it again.

INGREDIENTS:
½ jigger Midori
1 jigger Vodka
Juice of ½ Orange

PREPARATION:
Fill your shaker with ice. Add the Midori, Vodka, and Juice. Shake the mix vigorously. Strain over ice into a sour glass.

HONEYSUCKLE VINE

After one sip, you'll just want to be there.

INGREDIENTS:
1 jigger Rhum
1 t. Honey
1 t. Cream

PREPARATION:
Fill your shaker with ice. Add the Rhum, Honey, and Cream. Shake the mixture vigorously, then strain into a tin cup chalice.

HOODLUM DRINK

After one sip, you'll feel like you're missing a link.

INGREDIENTS:
1½ jiggers Rhum

Ginger Ale
Lime Slice, for garnish

PREPARATION:
Fill a highball glass with ice. Add the Rhum, then the
Ginger Ale. Swizzle. Garnish with the Slice of Lime.

HORNPIPE

After one sip, you'll dance across the decks.

INGREDIENTS:
1 jigger Gin
2 t. Cherry Brandy
1 Egg White**
Cherry, for garnish

*** Due to the slight risk of Salmonella or other food-borne
illness, I always must recommend caution in consuming raw
egg whites. To reduce this risk, always use only clean, fresh,
grade A or AA eggs that have been properly refrigerated. Be
certain that their shells have remained intact and avoid contact
between the yolks or whites and the shell.*

PREPARATION:
Fill your bar glass with ice. Add all three ingredients.
Shake the mix vigorously until the white begins to froth.
Strain over ice into a sour glass. Garnish with the Cherry.

HULA GIRL

After one sip, you'll know how to face the music.

INGREDIENTS:
2 jiggers Leilani Rhum
Juice of ½ Lime
2 dashes of Simple Syrup*
Lime Wedge, for garnish

A recipe for preparing a Simple Syrup can be found in the Glossary.

PREPARATION:
Fill your shaker with ice. Add the Rhum, Juice, and Simple Syrup. Shake the mix vigorously. Strain over ice into a sour glass. Garnish with the Wedge of Lime.

A HURRICANE HISTORY LESSON

"It's Five O'Clock Somewhere" - from LIVE AT FENWAY PARK (2005)

While Katrina will always be remembered as the hurricane that nearly wiped New Orleans off the map in 2005, this other legendary hurricane is the one that put Pat O'Brien's Bar on the map in the first place. It's also the hurricane that "Moose" Brown had in mind when he wrote the lyrics to "It's Five O'Clock Somewhere."

Long before 2003's Country Song of the Year brought renewed attention to this drink, hundreds of thousands of people who'd been down St. Peter Street in the Big Easy already had become familiar with this fruity, red creation that takes its name from the distinctive glassware that resembles a hurricane lamp. And then most of those people took home with them their hurricane glass emblazoned with the name: Pat O'Brien's.

To this day, though, there are countless people of all generations who tend to confuse this Pat O'Brien either with the famous one who portrayed Knute Rockne on the silver screen, or even with the less famous other who hosted "The Insider" on the small screen. But make no mistake about it, Pat O'Brien has a signature cocktail.

This concoction was created during World War II, when most whiskeys were simply in short supply. In order to purchase just a single case of any whiskey, the liquor salesmen forced bar owners to purchase as many as fifty cases of the more plentiful rhum! So, O'Brien set out to create a recipe that would use up this overabundance of rhum. This, then, is that recipe.

HURRICANE

After one sip, you'll be tryin' to reason (whatever the season).

INGREDIENTS:
> *1 jigger Light Rhum*
> *1 jigger Dark Rhum*
> *2 jiggers Pineapple Juice*
> *2 jiggers Orange Juice*
> *¼ jigger Grenadine*
> *Pineapple Slice, for garnish*
> *Cherry, for garnish*

PREPARATION:
> Fill your bar glass with ice. Add all the ingredients. Shake the mix vigorously for about thirty seconds, then strain it into a hurricane glass. Garnish with the Slice of Pineapple and the Cherry.

- I -

IGUANA

After one sip, you'll slither around the floor.

INGREDIENTS:
> ½ jigger Vodka
> ½ jigger Tequila
> ¼ jigger Kahlúa
> 1 jigger Sour Mix*
>
> * A recipe for preparing a Sour Mix can be found in the Glossary.

PREPARATION:
> Fill your shaker with shaved ice. Add all four ingredients. Shake the mix vigorously for about thirty seconds. Strain over ice into a cocktail glass.

INCOMMUNICADO

After one sip, you'll be taking the long way home.

INGREDIENTS:
> 1 jigger American Whiskey
> 2 dashes Bitters
> 2 jiggers Ginger Ale

PREPARATION:
> Fill a rocks glass with ice. Pour in the Whiskey and the Bitters, then top off with Ginger Ale. Swizzle gently.

INDECISION (YES AND NO)

After one sip, you may or may not have a problem.

INGREDIENTS:
> *2 jiggers Brandy*
> *4 dashes Curaçao*
> *1 Egg White***
> *Orange Peel, for garnish*

> *** Due to the slight risk of Salmonella or other food-borne illness, I always must recommend caution in consuming raw egg whites. To reduce this risk, always use only clean, fresh, grade A or AA eggs that have been properly refrigerated. Be certain that their shells have remained intact and avoid contact between the yolks or whites and the shell.*

PREPARATION:
> Fill your bar glass with ice. Add the three ingredients. Shake them until the egg white begins to foam. Strain over ice into a sour glass. Garnish with the Twist of Orange.

INFLATION FIGHTER

After one sip, you'll wonder where your cash flow went.

INGREDIENTS:
> *1 jigger Midori*
> *Juice of ½ Lemon*
> *Lemon Peel, for garnish*

PREPARATION:
> Fill your shaker with shaved ice. Add the Midori and the Juice. Shake vigorously for a few seconds. Strain into a chilled cocktail glass. Garnish with the Twist of Lemon.

ISLANDER

After one sip, you'll see what makes you different.

INGREDIENTS:
>   1 jigger Banana Liqueur
>   1 jigger Cointreau
>   1 jigger Cream
>   Orange Peel, for garnish

PREPARATION:
>   Fill your bar glass with crushed ice. Add in the Banana
>   Liqueur, the Cointreau, and the Cream. Shake the mix
>   vigorously for about thirty seconds. Strain over ice into a
>   sour glass. Garnish with the Twist of Orange.

ISLAND FEVER

After one sip, you'll feel a bit sautéed.

INGREDIENTS:
>   1 jigger Dark Rhum
>   ½ jigger Maraschino Liqueur
>   1 t. Cointreau
>   1 t. Grenadine
>   Orange Peel, for garnish

PREPARATION:
>   Fill your shaker with ice. Add the ingredients. Shake the
>   mix vigorously for about thirty seconds. Strain into a
>   chilled cocktail glass. Garnish with the Twist of Orange.

- J -

JAMAICA BREEZE

After one sip, the night wind takes you just where you want.

INGREDIENTS:
> *1 jigger Light Jamaican Rhum*
> *1 t. Cherry Brandy*
> *2 jiggers Orange Juice*
> *1 jigger Ginger Beer*
> *Orange Slice, for garnish*

PREPARATION:
> Fill your shaker with shaved ice. Add the Rhum, Brandy, and Orange Juice. Shake the mix vigorously. Strain over ice into a rockas glass. Top off with Ginger Beer. Garnish with the Slice of Orange.

JAMAICA FAREWELL

After one sip, your head be on your way.

INGREDIENTS:
> *1 jigger Jamaican Rhum*
> *1 jigger Coffee Liqueur*
> *1 jigger Lime Juice*
> *Dash of Bitters*
> *Lime Slice, for garnish*

PREPARATION:

Fill your shaker with cracked ice. Add the Rhum, Coffee Liqueur, Lime Juice, and Bitters. Shake the mixture vigorously. Strain over ice into a rocks glass. Garnish with the Slice of Lime.

JAMAICA MISTAICA

After one sip, you'll think they've all gone haywire.

INGREDIENTS:

2 jiggers Jamaican Rhum
1 jigger Grenadine
3 dashes Maraschino
3 dashes Curaçao
Orange Peel, for garnish

PREPARATION:

Fill your bar glass with ice. Add the Rhum, Grenadine, Maraschino, and Curaçao. Stir gently, then strain into a chilled cocktail glass. Garnish with the Twist of Orange.

JAMAICAN

After one sip, you'll get Jah lost in the reggae, mon.

INGREDIENTS:

1 jigger Jamaican Rhum
1 jigger Kahlúa
Juice of 2 Limes
Dash of Angostura Bitters
7-Up

PREPARATION:

Fill your shaker with shaved ice. Add only the Rhum, Kahlúa, Lime Juice, and Bitters. Shake the mix vigorously, then strain over ice into a rocks glass. Top off with 7-Up.

JAMAICA WIND

After one sip, you'll be winded yourself.

INGREDIENTS:
> 1 jigger Dark Jamaican Rhum
> ½ jigger Kahlúa

PREPARATION:
> Add ice to a rocks glass. Add the Rhum and Kahlúa. Swizzle once or twice.

JILLIONAIRE

After one sip, you'll feel like a true lottery winner.

INGREDIENTS:
> 1 jigger Bourbon
> ½ jigger Cointreau
> ½ t. Grenadine
> 1 Egg White**

> ** Due to the slight risk of Salmonella or other food-borne illness, I always must recommend caution in consuming raw egg whites. To reduce this risk, always use only clean, fresh, grade A or AA eggs that have been properly refrigerated. Be certain that their shells have remained intact and avoid contact between the yolks or whites and the shell.

PREPARATION:
> Fill your bar glass with with ice. Add the ingredients. Shake the mixture until the white begins to foam. Strain over ice into a sour glass.

JIMMY'S DREAM

After one sip, you'll count all your blessings.

INGREDIENTS:
> 2 jiggers Brandy

1 jigger *Curaçao*
1 dash *Pernod*
Orange Slice, *for garnish*

PREPARATION:

Fill a bar glass with ice. Add all the ingredients. Stir thoroughly, then strain into a chilled cocktail glass. Garnish with the Slice of Orange.

JIVE-ASS SMILE

After one sip, you won't pronounce your Rs or Gs.

1 jigger *Cointreau*
1 jigger *Swedish Punsch*
1 jigger *Crème de Cassis*

PREPARATION:

Gently pour each ingredient into a pousse-café glass so that they layer, rather than mix together. This is best done by pouring each slowly over the back of a spoon and into the glass. The bottom layer is Cointreau; the middle layer, Swedish Punsch; and the top layer, Crème de Cassis.

JOLLY MON

After one sip, you won't care if anything is true.

INGREDIENTS:

1 jigger *Dark Rhum*
1 jigger *Coconut Rhum*
1 jigger *Cream of Coconut*
Shredded Coconut, *for garnish*

PREPARATION:

Fill your shaker with ice. Add the Rhums and the Cream of Coconut. Shake the mix vigorously for about thirty seconds, then strain over ice into a rocks glass. Garnish with just a few Shreds of Coconut.

JOLLY ROGER

After one sip, you'll feel like you were born 200 years too late.

INGREDIENTS:
> *1 jigger Dark Rhum*
> *1 jigger Banana Liqueur*
> *2 jiggers Lemon Juice*
> *Lemon Slice, for garnish*

PREPARATION:
> Fill your shaker with shaved ice. Add the ingredients. Shake the mix thoroughly, then strain over ice into a rocks glass. Garnish with the Slice of Lemon.

JUNIOR MINT

After one sip, you'll wonder whatever happened.

INGREDIENTS:
> *½ jigger White Peppermint Schnapps*
> *½ jigger Bailey's Irish Cream*
> *½ jigger Crème de Cacao*
> *1 jigger Cream*
> *Mint Sprig, for garnish*

PREPARATION:
> Fill your blender one-quarter with ice. Add in all four liquid ingredients. Blend on high for about thirty seconds. Strain into a chilled cocktail glass. Garnish with the Sprig of Mint.

- K -

Keno Player

After one sip, you'll try to win it all with one more bet.

Ingredients:
1 jigger Bourbon
½ jigger Curaçao
1 Egg white**
Dash Grenadine
Orange Peel, for Garnish

** Due to the slight risk of Salmonella or other food-borne
illness, I always must recommend caution in consuming raw
egg whites. To reduce this risk, always use only clean, fresh,
grade A or AA eggs that have been properly refrigerated. Be
certain that their shells have remained intact and avoid contact
between the yolks or whites and the shell.

Preparation:
Fill your bar glass with cracked ice. Add the Bourbon,
Curaçao, and Egg White. Shake the mixture until the egg
white begins to foam. Strain over ice into a sour glass.
Garnish with the Twist of Orange.

KEY LIME PIE

After one sip, you'll wish lunch could last forever.

INGREDIENTS:
1 jigger Licor 43
1 jigger Cream
1 jigger Sour Mix*
Lime Slice, for garnish

* A recipe for preparing a Sour Mix can be found in the Glossary.

PREPARATION:
Fill your shaker with cracked ice. Add the ingredients. Shake the mixture vigorously, then strain over ice into a rocks glass.

KING OF SOMEWHERE HOT

After one sip, you'll dance the night away like the locals do.

INGREDIENTS:
1 jigger Dark Rhum
½ jigger Crème de Banana
½ jigger Lemon Juice
½ jigger Orange Juice
½ jigger Pineapple Juice

PREPARATION:
Fill your shaker with crushed ice. Add the ingredients. Shake the mixture vigorously, then strain over ice into a rocks glass. Garnish with a Slice of Orange.

KING OF ZANZIBAR

After one sip, you'll be straddling the equator.

INGREDIENTS:
1½ jiggers Dry Vermouth

1 jigger Gin
Juice of ½ Lemon
1 t. Simple Syrup*
3 dashes Bitters
Lemon Slice, for garnish

* A recipe for a Simple Syrup can be found in the Glossary.

PREPARATION:
Fill your shaker with crushed ice. Add the ingredients. Shake the mix vigorously. Strain into a chilled cocktail glass. Garnish with the Slice of Lemon.

KINGSTON

After one sip, your head will be turning around.

INGREDIENTS:
2 jiggers Jamaican Rhum
1 jigger Gin
½ jigger Simple Syrup*
Juice of 1 Lime
Lime Slice, for garnish

* A recipe for preparing a Simple Syrup can be found in the Glossary.

PREPARATION:
Fill your shaker with cracked ice. Add in only the liquid ingredients. Shake the mix vigorously. Strain into a chilled cocktail glass. Garnish with the Slice of Lime.

K.I.S.S.

After one sip, you'll keep it simple, stupid.

INGREDIENTS:
½ jigger Kahlúa
½ jigger Irish Cream

PREPARATION:

Pour the Kahlúa into a shot glass. Slowly pour the Irish Cream over the back of a spoon so that it floats atop the layer of Kahlúa. Savor this as a sipping shot.

- L -

L.A. Haze

After one sip, you'll be beside yourself.

INGREDIENTS:
1 jigger Vodka
1 jigger Chambord
Juice of 1 Lemon
Juice of 1 Lime
Lemon Slice, for garnish

PREPARATION:
Fill your bar glass with cracked ice. Add in all of the
ingredients. Stir them gently, then strain into over ice into
a rocks glass. Garnish with the Slice of Lemon.

Lage Nom Ai

After one sip, you won't even know your own name.

INGREDIENTS:
2 jiggers Gin
½ jigger Brandy
½ jigger Triple Sec
Juice of ½ Orange
Ginger Ale
Orange Slice, for garnish

PREPARATION:

Add ice to a rocks glass. Add the first four ingredients. Stir once or twice. Top off with the Ginger Ale. Garnish with the Slice of Orange.

LANDFALL

After one sip, you'll be tryin' to make a little sense of it all.

INGREDIENTS:

1 jigger 151 Proof Rhum
2 t. Lime Juice
1 t. Grenadine
Lime Slice, for garnish

PREPARATION:

Fill your bar glass with cracked ice. Add in the liquid ingredients. Stir gently, then strain into a chilled cocktail glass. Garnish with the Slice of Lime.

LANDSHARK

After one sip, you'll show your big white teeth.

INGREDIENTS:

½ jigger Light Rhum
½ jigger Dark Rhum
½ jigger Spiced Rhum
1 jigger Pineapple Juice
Juice of 1 Lime
Lime Wedge, for garnish

PREPARATION:

Fill your shaker with ice. Add all the liquid ingredients. Shake the mixture vigorously, then strain over ice into a rocks glass. Garnish with the Wedge of Lime.

LAST MAN STANDING

After one sip, you'll want them to bring on a little bit more.

INGREDIENTS:
> 1 jigger American Whiskey
> 1 t. Fine Granulated Sugar
> 2 jiggers Milk
> Grated Nutmeg, for garnish

PREPARATION:
> Spoon the Sugar into the bottom of your shaker, then fill the shaker with ice. Add the Milk and the Whiskey. Shake the mix vigorously for about thirty seconds. Strain into a chilled cocktail glass. Dust with fresh Grated Nutmeg.

LAST MANGO

After one sip, you'll see that there's still so much to be done.

INGREDIENTS:
> 1 jigger Gin
> ¼ jigger Dry Vermouth
> ¼ jigger Sweet Vermouth
> 1 jigger Mango Nectar
> 3 dashes Grenadine

PREPARATION:
> Fill your shaker with crushed ice. Add together all the ingredients. Shake the mixture vigorously, then strain into a chilled cocktail glass.

LEAKY TIKI

After one sip, you'll be waiting for those flashbacks to come.

INGREDIENTS:
> 2 jiggers Dry Gin
> ½ jigger Pineapple Juice

¼ jigger Orange Juice
¼ jigger Curaçao
Orange Slice, for garnish

PREPARATION:
Fill a bar glass with ice. Add the Gin, Juices, and Curaçao. Stir thoroughly and strain into a chilled cocktail glass. Garnish with the Slice of Orange.

LICENSE TO CHILL

After one sip, you'll be fully certified to do nothing.

INGREDIENTS:
1 jigger Vodka
1 jigger Blue Curaçao
1 jigger Lemon Juice
Orange Slice, for garnish

PREPARATION:
Fill your shaker with crushed ice. Add the Vodka, Blue Curaçao, and Juice. Shake the mix vigorously. Strain over ice into a rocks glass. Garnish with the Slice of Orange.

LICENSE TO FLY

After one sip, you'll get the bartender's ear.

INGREDIENTS:
1 jigger English Gin
1 jigger Lillet
2 dashes Apricot Brandy
2 dashes Orange Brandy
Orange Peel, for garnish

PREPARATION:
Fill your shaker with ice. Add in all the liquid ingredients. Shake the mixture vigorously, then strain into a chilled cocktail glass. Garnish with the Twist of Orange.

LITTLE LATITUDE

After one sip, you won't know whether you're up or down.

INGREDIENTS:
> *1 jigger Tequila*
> *½ jigger Banana Liqueur*
> *½ jigger Lime Juice*
> *Lime Peel, for garnish*

PREPARATION:
> Fill your blender one-quarter with crushed ice. Add the liquid ingredients. Blend on high until smooth. Pour into a chilled cocktail glass. Garnish with the Twist of Lime.

LIVINGSTON SATURDAY NIGHT

After one sip, you'll be a rockin' and a rollin'.

INGREDIENTS:
> *1 jigger American Whiskey*
> *1 jigger Gin*
> *1 jigger White Crème de Menthe*
> *Juice of 1 Lemon*
> *Lemon Slice, for garnish*

PREPARATION:
> Fill your shaker with ice. Add the Whiskey, Gin, Crème de Menthe, and Juice. Shake the mixture vigorously. Strain over ice into a rocks glass. Garnish with the Slice of Lemon.

LONE EAGLE

After one sip, you'll thumb your nose at gravity.

INGREDIENTS:
> *1 jigger Gin*
> *½ t. Apricot Brandy*

½ t. *Cherry Brandy*
½ jigger *Lemon Juice*
Cherry, for garnish

PREPARATION:

Fill your shaker with ice. Add together the Gin, Brandies, and the Juice. Shake the mixture vigorously. Strain over ice into a cocktail glass. Garnish with the Cherry.

LONE PALM

After one sip, you'll be in the port of Indecision.

INGREDIENTS:

1 jigger *Dry Gin*
1 jigger *Light Rhum*
½ jigger *Cointreau*
½ jigger *Lime Juice*
Orange Slice, for garnish

PREPARATION:

Fill your shaker with ice. Add together the Gin, Rhum, Cointreau, and Juice. Shake the mixture, then strain over ice into a rocks glass. Garnish with the Slice of Orange.

LONG BEACH ICED TEA

After one sip, you'll move like a spruce goose.

INGREDIENTS:

½ jigger *Vodka*
½ jigger *Gin*
½ jigger *Rhum*
½ jigger *Triple Sec*
½ jigger *Sour Mix**
1 jigger *7-Up*
2 jiggers *Cranberry Juice*
Lemon Wedge, for garnish

A recipe for a Sour Mix can be found in the Glossary.

PREPARATION:
Fill a bar glass with cracked ice. Add together all the ingredients. Stir once or twice, then strain over ice into a collins glass. Garnish with the Wedge of Lemon.

LONGBOARD

After one sip, you'll hang off your own nose.

INGREDIENTS:
2 jiggers Rhum
1 jigger Blue Curaçao
2 jiggers Pineapple Juice
½ jigger Simple Syrup*
Orange Slice, for garnish

A recipe for a Simple Syrup can be found in the Glossary.

PREPARATION:
Fill your bar glass with cracked ice. Add the ingredients. Stir well. Strain over ice into a rocks glass. Garnish with the Slice of Orange.

LOUIS L'AMOUR

After one sip, you'll wonder how he would do it.

INGREDIENTS:
1 jigger American Whiskey
1 jigger Dry Vermouth
Orange Peel, for garnish

PREPARATION:
Fill your bar glass with crushed ice. Add the Whiskey and the Dry Vermouth. Stir one or twice, then strain over ice into a cocktail glass. Garnish with the Twist of Orange.

LOVE IN THE LIBRARY

After one sip, you'll know there are no rules.

INGREDIENTS:

1 jigger Cointreau
1 jigger Crème de Pamplemousse
1 jigger Brandy
Grapefuit Peel, for garnish

PREPARATION:

Fill your bar glass with cracked ice. Add the Cointreau. the Crème de Pamplemousse, and the Brandy. Stir once or twice. Strain into over ice into a cocktail glass. Garnish with the Twist of Grapefruit.

LUCKY STAR

After one sip, you'll know it's gonna be one of those days.

INGREDIENTS:

1 jigger Metaxa
1 jigger Galliano

PREPARATION:

Combine the Metaxa and the Galliano in a brandy snifter. Swirl the glass, once or twice, before sipping.

- M -

MAGNOLIA BLOSSOM

After one sip, you'll think all the world's a dream come true.

INGREDIENTS:
1 jigger Gin
½ jigger Cream
1 jigger Lemon Juice
Dash Grenadine
Lemon Peel, for garnish

PREPARATION:
Fill your shaker with cracked ice. Add the Gin, Cream, Juice, and Grenadine. Shake the mix vigorously for about thirty seconds. Strain into a chilled cocktail glass. Garnish with the Twist of Lemon.

MALIBU WAVE

After one sip, you'll feel wiped out.

INGREDIENTS:
1 jigger Tequila
½ jigger Triple Sec
1 t. Blue Curaçao

1½ jiggers Sour Mix*
Lime Slice, for garnish

*A recipe for preparing a Sour Mix can be found in the Glossary.

PREPARATION:
Fill your shaker with cracked ice. Add all the ingredients. Shake the mix vigorously for about thirty seconds. Strain over ice into chilled cocktail glass. Garnish with the Slice of Lime.

MAÑANA

After one sip, you'll really mean everything you say.

INGREDIENTS:
1 jigger Light Rhum
1 jigger Coconut Rhum
½ Mango, very ripe
½ Banana, very ripe
Juice of 1 Lime
Lime Slice, for garnish

PREPARATION:
Fill your blender one-quarter with ice. Add ingredients. Blend for about a minute or until very smooth. Pour into a chilled cocktail glass. Garnish with the Slice of Lime.

A MARGARITA HISTORY LESSON

"(Waistin' Away Again in) Margaritaville"
- from CHANGES IN LATITUDES, CHANGES IN ATTITUDES (1977)

Basically, this is the concoction that created the Americanos' taste for tequila back in the 1960s. Before this, tequila (which is technically a brandy) was known mostly just inside Mexico. Tax records in the Mexican town of Tequila noted that three barrels of "mezcal wine" had been shipped to Texas in 1873, and American troops in pursuit of Pancho Villa had brought some back in 1916. Still, folks north of the border had not quite taken to the taste of tequila. Even when there was a shortage of gin during World War II, the gringo interest in the Mexican spirit proved to be nothing more than a flirtation. Then California college students discovered the Margarita, and the rest (as they say) is history.

As for the creation of the drink itself, several bars and bartenders have staked out a claim. The Caliente Racetrack in Tijuana boasts of its origin around 1930, as does Bertita's bar in Tasca, Mexico. Later claims have been insisted upon not only by the Garci Crespo Hotel in Puebla, Mexico, around 1936 (where the bartender says he named the drink for his girlfriend), but also by a couple from San Antonio, Texas, who spent many an hour wasting away during the 1950s at the bar of the Flamingo Hotel in Acapulco, where they owned a home. (Her name, of course, was Margarita.) And not to be denied a piece of the legend is a restaurant in Los Angeles called The Tale of the Cock, where they claim to have created this recipe first during the Eisenhower Administration.

But the most documented story comes from one Danny Herrera, who owned Rancho La Gloria between Rosarito Beach and Tijuana. In the late 1940s, a showgirl named Marjorie King stopped there quite often, and she had a drinking "problem" of sorts: she was allergic to every form of booze except tequila, which she still needed to have mixed with something.

Among the many tequila experiments that Herrera tried was a concoction consisting of 3 parts white tequila, 2 parts Cointreau, and 1 part fresh lemon juice. These he shook together in a container of shaved ice, then served up in a short-stemmed glass rimmed with lemon juice and salt. This she liked, and so he gave the new drink the Spanish name for Marjorie: *Margarita*.

Whether any of these claims is fiction or fact really matters not at all. What does matter, though, is that there are certain ingredients which *must* be in this cocktail. Anything either more, or less makes the concoction something else. That said, what follows is the true recipe, as well as some others that are simply nonsense.

MARGARITA (BASIC)

After one sip, you'll admit it's your own damn fault.

INGREDIENTS:

1 jigger White (Blanco) Tequila
2 jiggers Gold (Oro) Tequila
2 jiggers Triple Sec
1 jigger Lime Juice
2 t. Coarse Salt
1 Lime Wedge, for garnish

[Note: Triple Sec, Cointreau, Grand Marnier, and Curaçao are all orange-flavored liqueurs that are interchangeable in this recipe.]

PREPARATION:

First, salt the rim of your glass by placing coarse salt in a shallow dish, rubbing the rim of the glass with lime, then dipping rim into the salt for a thorough coating around the edge. Generally, this glass is some variation of a cock-tail glass, but a rocks glass is also an acceptable piece of barware.

Next, fill your shaker with cracked ice. Add the 3 jiggers of Tequila, the 2 jiggers of Triple Sec, and the 1 jigger of Lime Juice. This is your 3:2:1 ratio of Tequila to Orange Liqueur to Lime Juice. Shake the mix vigorously for about thirty seconds. Strain (over ice, if you wish) into the salt-rimmed glass. Garnish with the Wedge of Lime.

MARGARITA (FROZEN)

After one sip, you'll have the help you need to hang on.

INGREDIENTS:

1 jigger White (Blanco) Tequila
2 jiggers Gold (Oro) Tequila
2 jiggers Triple Sec
1 jigger Lime Juice

2 t. Coarse Salt
1 Lime Wedge, for garnish

[Note: The only real distinctions between a Basic and a Frozen Margarita are the blender and the glassware.]

PREPARATION:

First, salt the rim of your glass by placing coarse salt in a shallow dish, rubbing the rim of the glass with lime, then dipping rim into the salt for a thorough coating around the edge. Generally, this glass is some variation of a cocktail glass, but it usually has a large capacity.

Next, fill your blender one-quarter with cracked ice. Add the 3 jiggers of Tequila, the 2 jiggers of Triple Sec, and the 1 jigger of Lime Juice. This is your 3:2:1 ratio of Tequila to Orange Liqueur to Lime Juice. Blend the mixture on medium until the concoction is smooth. Pour into the salt-rimmed glass. Garnish with the Wedge of Lime.

A PERFECT MARGARITA© HISTORY LESSON

At his home bar in 1980, artist Bart Jackson perfected the Margarita as a remedy to South Carolina's "blue laws" that prohibited the sale of any booze on a Sunday. After one of Bart's friends told him of Jimmy's quest for the "Perfect Margarita," Bart illustrated "The Road to the Perfect Margarita," then sent it off to Margaritaville.

The rest is history. Or, should we say, the *recipe* is history: t-shirts, postcards, and a page in *The Parrothead Handbook* included in Jimmy's boxed set of CDs.

Meanwhile, back in Mt. Pleasant, Bart's copyrighted concoction is still served at his home bar: "Oh, at Lana's." If Bart won't let you in, here's his remedy for the blues.

INGREDIENTS:

Juice of 2 Lime Wedges
1 jigger Jose Cuervo 1800 Tequila
¼ jigger Cuervo White Tequila

¾ jigger Rose's Lime Juice
¼ jigger Bols Triple Sec
Splash Bols Orange Curaçao
2 t. Coarse Salt
1 Lime Wedge, for garnish

PREPARATION:
Fill your shaker with broken cubed ice. Squeeze 2 fresh Lime Wedges into shaker. Savor the fresh Lime aroma. *Aaaaaahhhhhh!* Add Cuervo 1800. Sniff the cork. Add the Cuervo White if you wish. (White for the bite!) Add Rose's Lime Juice. Add the Triple Sec. Add a splash of Orange Curaçao (*Shhh*...secret ingredient!)

Shake vigorously and strain over fresh ice into a salted glass. Garnish with juice of remaining wedge of Lime.

[Note: Thanks, Bart! - O.N.]

BLUE MARGARITA

Prepare BASIC or FROZEN using Blue Curaçao as your Orange flavor.

GOLD MARGARITA

Prepare BASIC or FROZEN using 3 parts of Gold (Oro) Tequila without any White (Blanco) Tequila.

FRUIT MARGARITA

Prepare BASIC or FROZEN using ½ cup of fruit along with ½ jigger of a matching liqueur in place of any orange-flavored liqueur. For example, a (so-called) Strawberry Margarita would match ½ jigger Strawberry Liqueur with ½ cup of Strawberries. (And though you might call it a Margarita, it really ain't! So, just get over it.)

MEA CULPA

After one sip, you'll act like one of those crazy-ass people.

INGREDIENTS:
1 t. Sugar
Juice of ½ Lemon
Juice of ½ Orange
Burgundy or Claret
Several dashes of Rhum
Orange Slice, for garnish

PREPARATION:
Spoon the Sugar into a collins glass, then fill the glass halfway with ice. Add the juices. Top with Burgundy or Claret. Add several dashes of Rhum. Swizzle. Garnish with the Slice of Orange.

MEMPHIS BELLE

After one sip, you'll know that your wild days are through.

INGREDIENTS:
1 jigger Brandy
½ jigger Southern Comfort
Juice of 1 Lemon
3 dashes Orange Bitters

PREPARATION:
Fill your shaker with cracked ice. Add the ingredients. Shake the mixture vigorously, then strain into a chilled cocktail glass. Garnish with the Slice of Orange.

MERMAID

After one sip, you won't have a leg to stand on.

INGREDIENTS:
2 jiggers Gin

Juice of 2 Lemons
½ jigger Crème de Menthe
Dash Angostura Bitters
Lemon Peel, for garnish

PREPARATION:

Fill your shaker with crushed ice. Add in the ingredients. Shake the mix vigorously for about thirty seconds. Strain into a chilled cocktail glass. Garnish with the Twist of Lemon.

MEXICAN CUTIE

After one sip, you won't have a clue.

INGREDIENTS:

1 jigger Tequila
Juice of ½ Lemon
4 dashes Grenadine
½ jigger Club Soda
Lemon Slice, for garnish

PREPARATION:

Fill your shaker with cracked ice. Add in the first three ingredients. Shake the mix vigorously for about thirty seconds. Strain into a chilled cocktail glass. Top off with the Club Soda. Garnish with the Slice of Lemon.

MIGRATION

After one sip, you'll stay contented most of the time.

INGREDIENTS:

1 jigger Rhum
½ jigger Unsweetened Grapefruit Juice
½ jigger Orange Juice
¼ jigger Curaçao
Orange Peel, for garnish

PREPARATION:

Fill your shaker with cracked ice. Add in the ingredients. Shake the mixture vigorously. Strain into a chilled cocktail glass. Garnish with the Slice of Orange.

MILKSHAKE IN MOTION

After one sip, you'll be livin' your life like a song.

INGREDIENTS:

1 jigger Bourbon
1 jigger Dark Rhum
1 jigger Milk

PREPARATION:

Fill your blender one-quarter with shaved ice. Add in the Bourbon, Dark Rhum. and Milk. Blend on medium until smooth. Pour over ice into a rocks glass.

MISSOULA OYSTER

After one sip, you'll find things better off than you feared.

INGREDIENTS:

½ jigger Cognac
1 T. Vinegar
1 T. Worcestershire
1 T. Ketchup
1 T. Angostura Bitters
*1 Egg Yolk***
Dash Cayenne Pepper

** Due to the slight risk of Salmonella or other food-borne illness, I always must recommend caution in consuming raw egg yolks. To reduce this risk, always use only clean, fresh, grade A or AA eggs that have been properly refrigerated. Be certain that their shells have remained intact and avoid contact between the yolks or whites and the shell.

PREPARATION:

Mix the first five ingredients without ice in a shot glass. Carefully, add the yolk without breaking. Dust with Cayenne. Bottoms up!

MISTER UTLEY

After one sip, you just won't know. Period.

INGREDIENTS:

2 jiggers Rhum
¾ jigger Pineapple Juice
3 dashes Grenadine
Pineapple Spear, for garnish

PREPARATION:

Fill your shaker with cracked ice. Add in the Rhum, Juice, and Grenadine. Shake the mixture vigorously. Strain into a chilled cocktail glass. Garnish with the Speak of Pineapple.

MOBILE HOME

After one sip, you'll walk as though your wheels have fallen off.

INGREDIENTS:

1 jigger Gin
½ jigger Dark Rhum
½ jigger Cointreau
Orange Slice, for garnish

PREPARATION:

Fill your shaker with cracked ice. Add in the Gin, Rhum, and Cointreau. Shake the mixture vigorously, then strain over ice into a chilled cocktail glass. Garnish with the Slice of Orange.

A MOJITO HISTORY LESSON

"Hooked in the Heart" - from TALES FROM MARGARITAVILLE (1993)

When I wrote the First Edition of this volume years ago, very few people in the States had ever heard of a Mojito. Today, though, it has become one of those trendy drinks. And like the Margarita and the Martini, mixologists everywhere have given into the pressures of liquor salesmen who have begged them to add whatever liquors they are trying to promote. As a result, the refreshing original Mojito has joined the Yuckarita and the Crapatini. So, let's toss those things out and get back to basics.

For starters, you should know that the Mojito is *not* pronounced moe-HEE-toe. Though the Cuban word has no other meaning than it is this one particular drink, there is no pronunciation of the letter J in the Cuban tongue. So, spread the word amongst the bee-yew-tee-full people. And that word is: moe-EE-toe.

Next, let's get the ingredients straight. The only stuff that goes into the Mojito is very similar to the basic ingredients in a couple of Hemingway's other favorite drinks: the Basic Daiquiri, as well as the Papa Dobles. In fact, Hemingway is supposed to have said: "My daiquiri at Floridita; my mojito at the Bodeguita," meaning that he enjoyed these two drinks at the bars of Havana's Floridita and La Bodeguita del Medio.

Its five essential, but basic ingredients aside, the other thing which sets this cocktail apart from all the rest is the colorful stirring utensil used by the Habaneros. Relying on neither a shaker, nor a blender, the proper preparation of this drink requires a wooden swizzle stick at the base of which radiates what has best been described as "a bird's foot." After the bartender adds the first four ingredients, this utensil is inserted to the bottom of the glass and the upright "leg" is rolled between the palms of both hands, thus blending the drink and ensuring that the sugar at the bottom is fully dissolved. Good luck finding one of those in the States!

Mojito

After one sip, you won't even taste the cube a sugar.

Ingredients:
> 1 jigger Light Rhum
> ½ jigger Lime Juice
> 1 t. Superfine Sugar
> Fresh Mint, crushed
> Club Soda
> Lime Wedge, for garnish

Preparation:
> Place the Fresh Mint in bottom of glass and then add the Sugar. Use a pestle to grind the Sugar into the Fresh Mint. This not only releases the essense of the Mint, but also serves to muddle the Sugar. Add the Lime Juice, Rhum, and Ice. Swizzle! Top off with Club Soda. Garnish with the Wedge of Lime. Now, that's a true Mojito!

Monsoon

After one sip, you'll have no ability to count your worth.

Ingredients:
> 1 jigger Light Rhum
> ½ jigger Coconut Rhum
> ½ jigger Grand Marnier
> ½ jigger Pineapple Juice
> ½ jigger Cranberry Juice
> 2 dashes Grenadine
> Orange Slice, for garnish

Preparation:
> Fill your bar glass with cracked ice. Add the first five ingredients. Stir thoroughly, then strain into a chilled cocktail glass. Add the Grenadine. Garnish with the Slice of Orange.

MOUSE IN ORLANDO

After one sip, you won't want to mess with the Big Cheese.

INGREDIENTS:
½ jigger Dark Rhum
½ jigger Coconut Rhum
½ jigger Crème de Banana
½ jigger Pineapple Juice
½ jigger Orange Juice
½ Jigger Grapefruit Juice
2 dashes Grenadine

PREPARATION:
Fill your shaker with crushed ice. Add all the ingredients. Shake the mix vigorously for about thirty seconds. Strain over ice into a rocks glass.

MUDSLIDE

After one sip, you'll think you have it all.

INGREDIENTS:
½ jigger Kahlúa
½ jigger Vodka
½ jigger Irish Cream
1½ jiggers Cream

PREPARATION:
Fill your blender one-quarter with cracked ice. Add in all the ingredients. Blend on medium until the mixture is smooth. Pour into a rocks glass.

MUMBO JUMBO

After one sip, you'll love the now.

INGREDIENTS:
1 jigger Dark Rhum

½ jigger Applejack
½ jigger Lemon Juice
½ t. Superfine Sugar
Dash Ground Cinnamon
Dash Ground Nutmeg

PREPARATION:

Add the Sugar to the bottom of your bar glass, then fill your with ice. Add the Rhum, Applejack, and Lemon Juice. Shake the mix vigorously for about thirty seconds. Strain into a chilled cocktail glass. Dust with freshly ground Cinnamon and freshly ground Nutmeg,

- N -

NATIVE TONGUE

After one sip, you'll keep it planted in your cheek.

INGREDIENTS:
1 jigger Dry Gin
1 jigger Grapefruit Juice
3 dashes Maraschino
Grapefruit Peel, for garnish

PREPARATION:
Fill your shaker with crushed ice. Add the Gin, Grapefruit Juice, and Maraschino. Shake the mix vigorously for about thirty seconds. Strain into a chilled cocktail glass. Garnish with the Twist of Grapefruit.

NAUTICAL WHEELER

After one sip, you'll be contented just livin' in ¾ time.

INGREDIENTS:
1 jigger Gin
½ jigger Sloe Gin
1 t. Grenadine
Lemon Peel, for garnish

PREPARATION:

Fill your shaker with ice. Add the Gin, the Sloe Gin, and the Grenadine. Shake the mixture, then strain into a chilled cocktail glass. Garnish with the Twist of Lemon.

NAVY GROG

After one sip, you'll find it's funny how it all works out.

INGREDIENTS:

½ jigger Light Rhum
½ jigger Dark Rhum
¼ jigger Falernum*
½ jigger Guava Nectar
½ jigger Pineapple Juice
½ jigger Orange Juice
1 jigger Sour Mix*
Lime Slice, for garnish

* A recipe for preparing Falernum, as well as a Sour Mix can be found in the Glossary.

PREPARATION:

Fill your shaker with cracked ice. Add all the ingredients. Shake the mixture vigorously, then strain over ice into a rocks glass. Garnish with the Slice of Lime.

NEW ORLEANS FIZZ

After one sip, you might well run into fruitcakes like you'd never believe.

INGREDIENTS:

1 jigger Gin
½ jigger Cream
1 t. Sugar
Juice of ½ Lime
Juice of ½ Lemon

1 Egg White**
3 dashes Orange Flower Water*
Soda Water
Orange Slice, for garnish

* A recipe for preparing Orange Flower Water can be found in the Glossary.

** Due to the slight risk of Salmonella or other food-borne illness, I always must recommend caution in consuming raw egg whites. To reduce this risk, always use only clean, fresh, grade A or AA eggs that have been properly refrigerated. Be certain that their shells have remained intact and avoid contact between the yolks or whites and the shell.

PREPARATION:
Fill your bar glass with shaved ice. Add only the first seven ingredients. Shake the mix vigorously for about thirty seconds or until the egg white begins to foam. Strain into a collins glass. Top off with Soda Water. Swizzle once or twice. Garnish with the Slice of Orange.

NEW ORLEANS PUNCH

After one sip, you'd better avoid those Bourbon Street bars.

INGREDIENTS:
½ jigger Raspberry Syrup
1 jigger Lemon Juice
½ jigger Jamaica Rhum
1 jigger Bourbon
1 jigger cold, strong Black Tea
Orange Slice, for garnish

PREPARATION:
Fill your shaker with ice. Add all the ingredients. Shake the mix vigorously for about thirty seconds. Strain over ice into a rocks glass. Garnish with the Slice of Orange.

NEXT EXPLOSION

After one sip, you'll get to work on your sense of survival.

INGREDIENTS:

> 2 jiggers Gin
> 1 jigger Campari
> 1 jigger Orange Juice
> 1 t. Grenadine
> 2 jiggers Ginger Ale
> Cherry, for garnish

PREPARATION:

> Fill your shaker with ice. Add in only the first four ingredients. Shake the mix vigorously for about thirty seconds. Strain over ice into a collins glass. Top off with Ginger Ale. Garnish with the Cherry.

OLD MANATEE

After one sip, your barnacle brain won't bend.

INGREDIENTS:
1 jigger Vodka
1 jigger Gin
½ jigger Kahlúa
Dash Pineapple Juice
Dash Grenadine
Dash Sour Mix*

* A recipe for preparing a Sour Mix can be found in the Glossary.

PREPARATION:
Fill your shaker with ice. Add in all the ingredients. Shake the mix vigorously, then strain over ice into a rocks glass.

OLD TRUTH TELLER

After one sip, you'll see it all eye to eye.

INGREDIENTS:
1 jigger Gin
½ jigger White Crème de Menthe
½ jigger Anisette
½ jigger Cream

PREPARATION:

Fill your shaker with crushed ice. Add all four ingredients. Shake the mix vigorously for about thirty seconds. Strain into a chilled cocktail glass.

ONE PARTICULAR HARBOR

After one sip, you can't explain likes of you.

INGREDIENTS:

1 jigger Light Rhum
1 jigger Crème de Noyaux
¼ jigger Southern Comfort
½ jigger Orange Juice
½ jigger Pineapple Juice
½ jigger Cream of Coconut
Orange Slice, for garnish

PREPARATION:

Fill your shaker with ice. Add the ingredients. Shake the mix vigorously, then strain into a sour glass. Garnish with the Slice of Orange.

ORANGE BLOOM

After one sip, you'll act like a bloomin' idiot, bud.

INGREDIENTS:

½ jigger Dry Gin
¼ jigger Sweet Vermouth
¼ jigger Cointreau
Cherry, for garnish

PREPARATION:

Fill your shaker with shaved ice. Add in all the ingredients. Shake the mix vigorously, then strain into a chilled cocktail glass. Garnish with the Cherry.

ORANGE BLOSSOM

After one sip, you'll be glad Anita Bryant doesn't sell orange juice anymore.

INGREDIENTS:
1 jigger Gin
½ jigger Simple Syrup*
2 jiggers Orange Juice
Orange Peel, for garnish

* A recipe for preparing a Simple Syrup can be found in the Glossary.

PREPARATION:
Fill your shaker with cracked ice. Add all three ingredients. Shake the mixture vigorously. Strain into a chilled cocktail glass. Garnish with the Twist of Orange.

ORION'S BELT

After one sip, you'll thank your lucky stars.

INGREDIENTS:
1 jigger Dark Rhum
½ jigger Kahlúa
Juice of ½ Lime
Lime Peel, for garnish

PREPARATION:
Fill your shaker with ice. Add the Rhum, Kahlúa, and the Lime Juice. Shake the mixture vigorously. Strain over ice into a sour glass. Garnish with the Twist of Lime.

- P -

Papa Dobles

After one sip, you'll drink the rest earnestly.

INGREDIENTS:
> *1 jigger Light Rhum*
> *Juice of 2 Limes*
> *Juice of ½ Grapefruit*

PREPARATION:
> Fill your bar glass with ice. Add the three ingredients. Stir thoroughly, then strain over ice into a rocks glass.

Paradise

After one sip, you'll understand that one sh*tty day is no different from another.

INGREDIENTS:
> *1 jigger Gin*
> *1 jigger Apricot Brandy*
> *1 jigger Orange Juice*
> *Orange Slice, for garnish*

PREPARATION:
> Fill your bar glass with ice. Add the ingredients. Stir thoroughly. Strain into a chilled cocktail glass. Garnish with the Slice of Orange.

PARAKEET'S CUSS

After one sip, you'll be ready to migrate.

INGREDIENTS:
> 1 jigger Vodka
> ½ jigger Melon Liqueur
> ½ jigger White Crème de Cacao
> 1 jigger Cream
> Orange Slice, for garnish

PREPARATION:
> Fill your shaker with cracked ice. Add the Vodka, Melon Liqueur, Crème de Cacao, and Cream. Shake the mix vigorously for about thirty seconds. Strain over ice into a rocks glass. Garnish with the Slice of Orange.

PASCAGOULA RUN

After one sip, you'll see just where it gets bizarre.

INGREDIENTS:
> 4 jiggers Dry Gin
> 1 jigger Lemon Juice
> 1 jigger Crème de Cassis
> Lemon Peel, for garnish

PREPARATION:
> Fill your shaker with shaved ice. Add the three ingredients. Shake the mixture vigorously for about thirty seconds, then strain into a chilled cocktail glass. Garnish with the Twist of Lemon.

PEANUT BUTTER CONSPIRACY

After one sip, you'll promise to pay everyone back.

INGREDIENTS:
> 1 jigger Peanut Rum Creme Liqueur

2 jiggers Crème de Cacao
1 jigger Cream

[Note: My original recipe for this cocktail in previous editions called for a jigger of the spirit called Peanut Lolita, which was produced by the Continental Distillery of Philadelphia. Along with their La Conga and Sevilla rhums, as well as Peanut Lolita, the distillery closed up its operations in the mid-1980s. Watch for some in an estate sale. 'Til then, Peanut Rum Creme Liqueur will do.]

PREPARATION:
Fill your shaker with cracked ice. Add the Peanut Rum Creme Liqueur, the Crème de Cacao, and the Cream. Shake the mix vigorously. Strain over ice into a rocks glass.

PENCIL THIN MOUSTACHE

After one sip, you could solve some mysteries, too.

INGREDIENTS:
2 jiggers Vodka
Juice of ½ Lemon
Ginger Beer
Lime Wedge, for garnish

PREPARATION:
Fill your shaker with cracked ice. Add only the first two ingredients, then shake the mixture vigorously. Strain over ice into a rocks glass. Top off with Ginger Beer. Garnish with the Wedge of Lime.

PERMANENT REMINDER

After one sip, your human nature will miscalculate.

INGREDIENTS:
1 jigger Dark Rhum
2 t. Dubonnet

3 dashes Grand Marnier
Lemon Slice, for Garnish

PREPARATION:
Fill your shaker with cracked ice. Add the ingredients. Shake the mix vigorously, then strain into a chilled cocktail glass. Garnish with the Slice of Lemon.

PIECE OF WORK

After one sip, you'll be who the hell you are.

INGREDIENTS:
2 jiggers American Whiskey
1 jigger Cream
Orange Slice, for garnish

PREPARATION:
Fill your shaker with shaved ice. Add the Whiskey and the Cream. Shake the mix vigorously. Strain over ice into a rocks glass. Garnish with the Slice of Orange.

PILOT BOAT

After one sip, you'll forget your brahma fear.

INGREDIENTS:
1 jigger Dark Rhum
½ jigger Banana Liqueur
Juice of 2 Limes
Lime Peel, for garnish

PREPARATION:
Fill your shaker with cracked ice. Add the Rhum, Banana Liqueur, and Juice. Shake the mix vigorously. Strain into a chilled cocktail glass. Garnish with the Twist of Lime.

PIÑA COLADA

After one sip, you'll forget you ever heard of Rupert Holmes.

INGREDIENTS:
1 jigger Rhum
1½ jiggers Pineapple Juice
½ jigger Cream of Coconut
½ jigger Cream
Pineapple Wedge, for garnish

PREPARATION:
Fill your blender one-quarter with ice. Add in the first four ingredients. Blend on medium until smooth. Pour into a frosted rocks glass. Garnish with the Wedge of Pineapple.

PIRATE

After one sip, you'll discover a new occupational hazard.

INGREDIENTS:
2 jiggers Dark Rhum
1 jigger Vermouth
Dash Angostura Bitters
Orange Peel, for garnish

PREPARATION:
Fill your bar glass with shaved ice. Add the ingredients. Stir well. Strain into a chilled cocktail glass.

PLANKWALK

After one sip, you'll be close to going over the edge.

INGREDIENTS:
1 jigger Dark Rhum
1 jigger Cranberry Juice
Juice of 1 Lime
Lime Wedge, for garnish

PREPARATION:

Fill your shaker with ice. Add the Rhum and Juices. Shake the mixture thoroughly. Strain over ice into a rocks glass. Garnish with the Wedge of Lime.

PLANTATION PUNCH

After one sip, you'll be glad you're not anywhere else but here.

INGREDIENTS:

1 jigger Southern Comfort
½ jigger Lemon Juice
½ jigger Rhum
1 t. Sugar
Soda Water
Orange Peel, for garnish

PREPARATION:

Place the Sugar in an old-fashioned glass, then add the Juice. Stir to dissolve. Add ice, along with the Southern Comfort, Rhum, and Soda. Swizzle once or twice. Garnish with the Twist of Orange.

PLANTER'S PUNCH (NO. 1)

After one sip, you'll be willing to work for peanuts.

INGREDIENTS:

2 jiggers Leilani Rhum
½ jigger Lime Juice
1 t. Sugar
Cherry, for garnish
Half slice of Orange, for garnish
Half slice of Lemon, for garnish
Half slice of Pineapple, for garnish

PREPARATION:

Fill your shaker with cracked ice. Add the Rhum, Juice,

and Sugar. Shake the mix vigorously. Strain over ice into rocks glass. Garnish with the fruit.

PLANTER'S PUNCH (NO. 2)

After one sip, you'll be ready to try another.

INGREDIENTS:

1 jigger Lime Juice
2 jiggers Simple Syrup*
3 jiggers Jamaica Rhum
2 jiggers Water
Cherry, for garnish
Orange Slice, for garnish

* A recipe for preparing a Simple Syrup can be found in the Glossary.

PREPARATION:

Fill a tall glass with ice. Add the ingredients Stir once or twice. Garnish with the Cherry and the Slice of Orange.

PURPLE PASSION

After one sip, you'll know it's good for your soul.

INGREDIENTS:

1 jigger Gin
2 jiggers Grape Juice
2 jiggers Grapefruit Juice
1 t. Sugar

PREPARATION:

Fill tall glass with ice. Add the Gin, the Juices, and the Sugar. Stir once or twice.

PYRO'S DELIGHT

After one sip, you'll put away your differences for a while.

INGREDIENTS:
> *1 jigger Rhum*
> *2 dashes Curaçao*
> *2 dashes Pernod*
> *Dash of Peychaud's Bitters*
> *1 Orange slice, for garnish*
> *1 Pineapple slice, for garnish*
> *1 Lemon Peel, for garnish*

PREPARATION:
> Fill your shaker with shaved ice. Add the Rhum, Curaçao, and Pernod. Shake the mix vigorously for about thirty seconds. Strain over ice into a rocks glass. Add the dash of Bitters. Garnish with the Slices of Orange and Pineapple, as well as the Twist of Lemon.

Q

QUARTERDECK

After one sip, you'll go fast enough to get there, but slow enough to see.

INGREDIENTS:
> 1 jigger Light Rhum
> 1 T. Sherry
> Juice of ½ Lime
> 1 Lime Peel, for garnish

PREPARATION:
> Fill your shaker with cracked ice. Add all three ingredients. Shake the mix vigorously for about thirty seconds. Strain into a chilled cocktail glass. Garnish with the Twist of Lime.

QUASAR

After one sip, your soul will be in the stars.

INGREDIENTS:
> 1 jigger Dark Rhum
> 1 jigger Vodka
> 1½ t. Lemon Juice
> 1½ t. Passion Fruit Juice
> 1 Lemon Peel, for garnish

PREPARATION:

Fill your shaker with ice. Add the Rhum, Vodka, and Juices. Shake the mix vigorously for about thirty seconds. Strain over ice into a rocks glass. Garnish with the Twist of Lemon.

QUIET NOISEMAKER

After one sip, you'll be pissin' off the old killjoys.

INGREDIENTS:

1½ jiggers Jamaican Rhum
1 t. Superfine Sugar
½ jigger Lemon Juice
2 dashes Orange Bitters
7-Up
Orange Peel, for garnish

PREPARATION:

In the bottom of a highball glass, dissolve the Sugar with the Rhum. Add the Lemon Juice, Ice, and Bitters. Stir once or twice. Fill with 7-Up. Garnish with the Twist of Orange.

- R -

Ragtop Day

After one sip, you'll throw all your cares away.

INGREDIENTS:
1 jigger Light Rhum
½ jigger Peach Schnapps
2 jiggers Peach Nectar
1 jigger Orange Juice
Juice of ½ Lemon
Orange Peel, for garnish

PREPARATION:
Fill your blender one-quarter with ice. Add in all five ingredients. Blend on low until smooth. Pour into a frosted goblet. Garnish with the Twist of Orange.

Railroad Lady

After one sip, you'll be tryin' to get home again.

INGREDIENTS:
1 jigger Whiskey
1 t. Powdered Sugar
Juice of 1 Lemon
Ginger Ale
Lemon Peel, for garnish

PREPARATION:

Spoon the Sugar into a collins glass, then stir in the Whiskey and Juice. Add three ice cubes. Fill with Ginger Ale. Swizzle. Garnish with the Twist of Lemon.

RAMOS FIZZ

After one sip, you'll be looking for that hidden track.

INGREDIENTS:

1 jigger Gin
Juice of ½ Lemon
Juice of ½ Lime
1 jigger Heavy Cream
½ t. Sugar
2 to 3 drops Orange Flower Water*
1 Egg White**
Club Soda
Orange Peel, for garnish

* A recipe for preparing an Orange Flower Water can be found in the Glossary.

** Due to the slight risk of Salmonella or other food-borne illness, I always must recommend caution in consuming raw egg whites. To reduce this risk, always use only clean, fresh, grade A or AA eggs that have been properly refrigerated. Be certain that their shells have remained intact and avoid contact between the yolks or whites and the shell.

PREPARATION:

Fill your bar glass with crushed ice. Add in the Gin, Juices, Cream. Sugar, Orange Flower Water, and the Egg White. Shake the mix vigorously for at least a minute or until the Egg White begins to foam. Strain into a chilled collins glass, Top off with Club Soda. Garnish with the Twist of Orange.

RASTAMAN'S REVENGE

After one sip, this time you'll KNOW you've seen Marley's ghost.

INGREDIENTS:
1 jigger Gin
½ jigger Dark Rhum
½ jigger Ruby Port
Juice of ½ Orange
Juice of ½ Lime
½ t. Superfine Sugar
Orange Slice, for garnish

PREPARATION:
Spoon the Sugar into your shaker, then fill it with crushed ice. Add the Gin, Rhum, and the Juices. Shake the mixture vigorously for about thirty seconds. Strain into a chilled cocktail glass. Garnish with the Slice of Orange.

REGGAE REEFER

After one sip, you'll not be able to stop this madness.

INGREDIENTS:
1 jigger Vodka
½ jigger Crème de Banana
1 jigger Orange Juice
½ jigger Grapefruit Juice
½ jigger Pineapple Juice
Dash Orange Bitters
4 dashes Grenadine
Orange Slice, for garnish
Pineapple Wedge, for garnish

PREPARATION:
Fill your shaker with crushed ice. Add all the ingredients. Shake Shake the mix vigorously. Strain over ice into a rocks glass. Garnish with the Slice of Orange and the Wedge of Pineapple.

RED SNAPPER

After one sip, you'll have trouble making landfall.

INGREDIENTS:

½ jigger Amaretto
½ jigger Crown Royal
½ jigger Cranberry Juice
Orange Peel, for garnish

PREPARATION:

Fill your shaker with crushed ice. Add the Amaretto, Crown Royal, and Cranberry Juice. Stir thoroughly. Strain into a chilled cocktail glass. Garnish with the Twist of Orange.

REMITTANCE MAN

After one sip, you'll be breaking all the rules.

INGREDIENTS:

1 jigger Light Rhum
1 jigger Dark Rhum
½ jigger Curaçao
¼ jigger Simple Syrup*
¼ jigger Orgeat*
Juice of 1 Lime
Lime Peel, for garnish

* A recipe for preparing a Simple Syrup and for Orgeat can be found in the Glossary.

PREPARATION:

Fill your shaker with crushed ice. Add the two Rhums, the Curaçao, the Simple Syrup, the Orgeat, and the Lime Juice. Stir thoroughly, then strain into a chilled cocktail glass. Garnish with the Twist of Lime.

RHETT BUTLER

After one sip, frankly, you won't give a damn.

INGREDIENTS:

1 jigger Southern Comfort
Juice of ¼ Lime
Juice of ¼ Lemon
1 t. Curaçao
½ t. Sugar
Orange Slice, for garnish

PREPARATION:

Spoon the Sugar into your shaker, then fill with cracked ice. Add the Southern Comfort, Juices, and the Curaçao. Shake the mix vigorously for about thirty seconds. Strain into a chilled cocktail glass. Garnish with the Slice of Orange.

RICKY RICARDO

After one sip, you'll love feeling loosey.

INGREDIENTS:

1 jigger Light Rhum
½ jigger Mandarin Liqueur
1 jigger Pineapple Juice
1 jigger Cream of Coconut
1 Orange Wedge, peeled
Orange Slice, for garnish

PREPARATION:

Fill your blender one-quarter with cracked ice. Add first 4 ingredients, plus one Wedge of Orange (peeled). Blend about a minute on high until smooth, then pour into a highball glass. Garnish with the Slice of Orange.

RIDDLE IN THE SAND

After one sip, you'll know that answers are the easy part.

INGREDIENTS:
 1 jigger Blended Whiskey
 ½ jigger Cherry Brandy
 1 jigger Cranberry Juice
 Orange Slice, for garnish

PREPARATION:
 Fill a rocks glass with ice. Add the Whiskey, Brandy, and Juice. Stir once or twice. Garnish with the Slice of Orange.

ROMAN CANDLE

After one sip, you'll be ready to paint up the sky.

INGREDIENTS:
 1 jigger Campari
 1 jigger Cranberry Juice
 Juice of ¼ Lemon
 Lemon Peel, for garnish

PREPARATION:
 Fill a rocks glass with ice. Add the Campari and both Juices. Stir once or twice. Garnish with the Twist of Lemon.

RUMRUNNER

After one sip, you'll discover another occupational hazard.

INGREDIENTS:
 ½ jigger Light Rhum
 ½ jigger Dark Rhum
 ½ jigger Blackberry Brandy
 ½ jigger Crème de Banana
 ½ jigger Orange Juice

1 jigger Sour Mix*
¼ jigger Lime Juice
¼ jigger Pineapple Juice
¼ jigger Grenadine
¼ jigger 151 Proof Rum
Lime Wedge, for garnish

* A recipe for preparing a Sour Mix can be found in the Glossary.

PREPARATION:

Fill your shaker with crushed ice. Add only the first nine ingredients. Stir thoroughly, then strain over ice into a rocks glass. Float the 151 Rhum on top. Garnish with the Wedge of Lime.

- S -

Sag Harbor Iced Tea

After one sip, you'll be high over Long Island Sound.

INGREDIENTS:

> ½ jigger Vodka
> ½ jigger Gin
> ½ jigger Rhum
> ½ Triple Sec
> 2 jiggers Sour Mix*
> 1 jigger Coca Cola
> Orange Slice, for garnish
>
> *A recipe for preparing a Sour Mix can be found in the Glossary.*

PREPARATION:

> Fill your shaker with cracked ice. Add the Vodka, Gin, Rhum, Triple Sec, and the Sour Mix. Stir thoroughly, then strain into a collins glass. Add the Cola and swizzle. Garnish with the Slice of Orange.

Salome

After one sip, you'll take your drum and beat it.

Ingredients:
> ½ jigger Gin
> ½ jigger Dry Vermouth
> 1 T. Sweet Vermouth
> Lemon Peel, for garnish

Preparation:
> Fill your shaker with crushed ice. Add the Gin and both Vermouths. Stir gently, then strain into a chilled cocktail glass. Garnish with the Twist of Lemon.

Salty Dog

After one sip, you'll catch the next tide back where you belong.

Ingredients:
> 2 jiggers Vodka
> 4 jiggers Grapefruit Juice
> Salt, for rimming glass

Preparation:
> First, salt the rim of your rocks glass by placing coarse salt in a shallow dish, rubbing the rim of the glass with grapefruit, then dipping rim into the salt to coat the edge.
>
> Add ice to the glass, then pour in the Vodka and Grapefruit Juice. Swizzle.

Sandbar

After one sip, you'll be payin' for your sins on earth.

Ingredients:
> 1 jigger Gin
> ½ jigger Orange Juice
> Juice of ½ Lime

Ginger Ale
Orange Slice, for garnish

PREPARATION:

Fill your shaker with ice. Add only the Gin and the Juices. Shake the mix vigorously for about thirty seconds. Strain over ice into collins glass. Fill with Ginger Ale. Swizzle. Garnish with the Slice of Orange.

SAN JUAN COOLER

After one sip, you'll be charging everything.

INGREDIENTS:

2 jiggers Puerto Rican Rhum
½ jigger Lemon Juice
2 jiggers Pineapple Juice
Quinine Water
Lemon Slice, for garnish

PREPARATION:

Fill a collins glass with ice. Pour in the Rhum and the Juices, then stir. Top off with Quinine. Swizzle. Garnish with the Slice of Lemon.

SANTIAGO

After one sip, you'll be hooked.

INGREDIENTS:

2 jiggers Rhum
2 dashes Grenadine
4 dashes Lime Juice
Lime Slice, for garnish

PREPARATION:

Fill your bar glass with ice. Add the Rhum, Grenadine, and the Lime Juice. Stir thoroughly and strain into a chilled cocktail glass. Garnish with the Slice of Lime.

SCARLETT O'HARA

After one sip, you'll be glad that tomorrow is another day.

INGREDIENTS:

> *1½ jiggers Cranberry Juice*
> *1 jigger Lime Juice*
> *4 jiggers Southern Comfort*
> *Lime Slice, for garnish*

PREPARATION:

Fill your shaker with crushed ice. Add the Juices and the Southern Comfort. Shake the mix vigorously for about thirty seconds. Strain into a chilled cocktail glass. Garnish with the Slice of Lime.

SECOND WIND

After one sip, you'll hear your words start comin' out wrong.

INGREDIENTS:

> *2 jiggers White Wine*
> *1 jigger Cranberry Juice*
> *½ jigger Peach Schnapps*
> *½ jigger Simple Syrup**
> *½ jigger Sour Mix**
> *Club Soda*
> *Peach Wedge, for garnish*
>
> ** A recipe for preparing a Simple Syrup and for a Sour Mix can be found in the Glossary.*

PREPARATION:

Pour the first five ingredients into a collins glass. Stir once or twice. Add ice to your glass, then top off with the Club Soda. Garnish with the Wedge of Peach.

SEMI-TRUE STORY

After one sip, you'll think it's too much tequila . . . or not quite enough.

INGREDIENTS:
½ jigger Light Rhum
½ jigger Tequila
½ jigger Vodka
2 jiggers Pineapple Juice
1 jigger Cream of Coconut
2 t. Milk
Dash Grenadine
Cherry, for garnish

PREPARATION:
Fill your shaker with crushed ice. Add all the ingredients. Shake the mix vigorously for about thirty seconds. Strain over ice into a collins glass. Garnish with the Cherry.

SEVENTH SISTER

After one sip, you'll be calling through the light years.

INGREDIENTS:
2 jiggers Dark Rhum
Juice of ½ Lime
2 dashes of Simple Syrup*
Lime Wedge, for garnish

* A recipe for preparing a Simple Syrup can be found in the Glossary.

PREPARATION:
Fill your shaker with crushed ice. Add the Rhum, Juice, and Simple Syrup. Shake the mix vigorously. Strain into a chilled cocktail glass. Garnish with the Wedge of Lime.

SEX ON THE BEACH

After one sip, you'll be somewhere down Montserrat way.

INGREDIENTS:

1 jigger Vodka
½ jigger Melon Liqueur
½ jigger Raspberry Liqueur
1 jigger Pineapple Juice
1 jigger Cranberry Juice
Orange Slice, for garnish

PREPARATION:

Fill your shaker with crushed ice. Add together all the ingredients. Shake the mix vigorously for about thirty seconds. Strain over ice into a collins glass. Garnish with the Slice of Orange.

SHARK BITE

After one sip, you'll feel like everyone's chum.

INGREDIENTS:

1 jigger Dark Rhum
2 jiggers Orange Juice
½ jigger Sour Mix*
½ jigger Grenadine
Orange Slice, for garnish

* A recipe for preparing a Sour Mix can be found in the Glossary.

PREPARATION:

Fill your blender one-quarter with crushed ice. Add in all the ingredients. Blend about one minute on high until smooth, then pour into a frosted goblet. Garnish with the Slice of Orange.

SHARK'S TOOTH

After one sip, you'll be showin' them pearly whites.

INGREDIENTS:

1 jigger Dark Rhum
½ jigger Lime Juice
½ jigger Lemon Juice
¼ jigger Grenadine
Club Soda
Cherry, for garnish

PREPARATION:

Fill your shaker with crushed ice. Add the Rhum, Juices, and Grenadine. Shake the mix vigorously for about thirty seconds. Strain over ice into a collins glass. Top off with Club Soda. Garnish with the Cherry.

SHIPWRECK

After one sip, you'll just want to lounge around.

INGREDIENTS:

1 jigger Sherry
¼ jigger Whiskey
2 dashes Rhum
2 dashes Orange Bitters
Orange Slice, for garnish

PREPARATION:

Fill your shaker with crushed ice. Add the Sherry, Whiskey, Rhum, and Orange Bitters. Shake the mix vigorously for about thirty seconds. Strain into a chilled cocktail glass. Garnish with the Slice of Orange.

SIMPLE COMPLICATION

After one sip, you'll know it's all right to be crazy.

INGREDIENTS:
>1 jigger Vodka
>½ jigger Blue Curaçao
>2 jiggers Orange Juice
>2 jiggers Pineapple Juice
>Cherry, for garnish

PREPARATION:
>Fill your shaker with crushed ice. Add in the four ingredients. Shake the mix vigorously for about thirty seconds. Strain over ice into a rocks glass. Garnish with the Cherry.

A SINGAPORE SLING HISTORY LESSON

"ALTERED BOY" - from FAR SIDE OF THE WORLD (2002)

The number of people in this world who actually know the defining ingredients in any sling recipe probably equals the number of people who actually know what country Singapore is in. So, it only complicates matters when we try to discuss the issues behind the legendary Singapore Sling.

Just for starters, though, a true sling recipe has either whiskey or gin or brandy mixed with lemon juice, sugar, and soda water. Served in a tall glass, a sling could be either hot or cold. And that brings us to Singapore, and you know where that is. Singapore is in Singapore that same way that the Vatican is in the Vatican and Monaco is in Monaco. Singapore is one of only four city-states remaining in the world. (The other is San Marino, and I'm sure you pick *that* out on the map, too.)

But if you think all that is confusing, just wait 'til we get through with this recipe for the Singapore Sling. The lore behind this concoction says that it was created at the Long Bar of the Raffles Hotel in Singapore by a bartender named Ngiam Tong Boon. Some say it was 1915; others, 1913; still more, 1910. What does that matter, though, if no one can agree upon its ingredients?

Apparently, Ngiam wrote down the recipe and stored it in the Long Bar's safe; however, it has been misplaced along the way. And so, the hotel has tried to recreate the drink based upon the recollection of employees, patrons, and any local writings of that time. As a result, there is the Singapore Sling served at the Raffles and then there is the Singapore Sling served elsewhere throughout Singapore. Ironically, the Long Bar's recipe contains neither lemon juice, nor soda water. Thus, trekking to Singapore's Long Bar for the sake of enjoying this historic concoction is like trekking to Havana for a mojito or only-God-knows-where for a genuine Margarita. Chances are, you'll be served some disappointing commercial recipe, and you'd be better off mixing one on the fantail of your own vessel.

SINGAPORE SLING (RAFFLES' LONG BAR)

INGREDIENTS:

1 jigger Gin
½ jigger Heering Cherry Liqueur
¼ jigger D.O.M Benedictine
¼ jigger Cointreau
4 jiggers Pineapple juice
½ jigger fresh lime juice
¼ jigger Grenadine
Dash of Angostura Bitters
Cherry, for garnish
Pineapple Chunk, for garnish
Orange Slice, for garnish

PREPARATION:

Fill your shaker with crushed ice. Add in the eight ingredients. Shake the mix vigorously for about thirty seconds. Strain straight up into a collins glass. Garnish with the Cherry, with the Pineapple, and with the Slice of Orange.

SINGAPORE SLING (STANDARD)

INGREDIENTS:

1½ jiggers Gin
1½ jiggers Lemon Juice
½ t. Powdered Sugar
1½ jiggers Club Soda
½ jigger Cherry Brandy
Lemon Slice, for garnish
Cherry for garnish

PREPARATION:

Fill your shaker with cracked ice. Add the Gin, Juice, and the Sugar. Shake the mix vigorously. Strain over ice into a collins glass. Float the Cherry Brandy on the top, Garnish with the Slice of Lemon and the Cherry.

SINK OR SWIM

After one sip, you'll be in over your head.

INGREDIENTS:

1 jigger Dry Gin
1 jigger Dry Vermouth
2 dashes Orange Bitters
2 dashes Maraschino
Orange Peel, for garnish

PREPARATION:

Fill your shaker with crushed ice. Add the ingredients. Stir thoroughly. Strain into a chilled cocktail glass. Garnish with the Twist of Orange.

SKIP WILEY

After one sip, you'll feel crazy and dangerous.

INGREDIENTS:

1 jigger Southern Comfort

> *2 t. Anisette*
> *1 T. Orange Juice*
> *2 t. Lemon Juice*
> *Orange Slice, for garnish*

PREPARATION:

Fill your shaker with cracked ice. Add the Southern Comfort, Anisette, and Juices. Shake the mix vigorously for about thirty seconds. Strain over ice into a rocks glass. Garnish with the Slice of Orange.

SKY KING

After one sip, your crown will be flying.

INGREDIENTS:

> *1 jigger Vodka*
> *1 jigger Cointreau*
> *Juice of 2 limes*
> *Lime Peel, for garnish*

PREPARATION:

Fill your shaker with ice. Add the Vodka, Cointreau, and Juices. Shake the mix vigorously. Strain into a chilled cocktail glass. Garnish with the Twist of Lime.

SLEEPLESS KNIGHT

After one sip, you'll be raising hell tonight.

INGREDIENTS:

> *1 jigger Rhum*
> *Juice of ½ Lime*
> *1 t. Green Crème de Menthe*
> *1 t. Simple Syrup**
> *½ t. Curaçao*
> *Lime Slice, for garnish*

> ** A recipe for a Simple Syrup can be found in the Glossary.*

PREPARATION:

Fill your shaker with shaved ice. Add all five ingredients. Shake the mix vigorously for about thirty seconds. Strain over ice into a rocks glass. Garnish with the Slice of Lime.

SMART WOMAN (IN A REAL SHOT GLASS)

After one sip, you'll get the urge to merge.

INGREDIENTS:

1 jigger Brandy
½ jigger Light Rhum
1 t. Curaçao
1 t. Grenadine
1 t. Lime Juice

PREPARATION:

Fill your shaker with crushed ice. Add the Brandy, Rhum, Curaçao, Grenadine, and Lime Juice. Shake the mix vigorously for about thirty seconds. Strain into a tall shot glass. Savor the flavor rather than shooting this drink.

SNAKE BITE

After one sip, you'll party just like Bubba does.

INGREDIENTS:

½ jigger Wild Turkey
½ jigger Peppermint Schnapps

PREPARATION:

Fill your shaker with crushed ice. Add the Wild Turkey and Schnapps. Shake the mix vigorously for about thirty seconds. Strain into a tall shot glass. Savor the flavor rather than shooting this drink.

SNUFF QUEEN

After one sip, you won't believe it's true.

INGREDIENTS:
> *1 jigger Bourbon*
> *1 jigger Light Rhum*
> *½ jigger Triple Sec*
> *Orange Peel, for garnish*

PREPARATION:
> Fill your shaker with ice. Add the Bourbon, Rhum, and Triple Sec. Shake the mix vigorously. Strain into a chilled cocktail glass. Garnish with the Twist of Orange.

SOMBRERO

After one sip, you'll be ready to siesta.

INGREDIENTS:
> *1 jigger Kahlúa*
> *1 jigger Cream*

PREPARATION:
> Fill your shaker with crushed ice. Add the Kahlúa and the Cream. Shake the mix vigorously for about thirty seconds. Strain over ice into a rocks glass.

SOUTHERN CROSS

After one sip, you'll be reminded of where you are.

INGREDIENTS:
> *½ jigger Gin*
> *2 jiggers Orange Juice*
> *1 t. Kirschwasser*
> *1 t. Triple Sec*
> *1 t. Lemon Juice*
> *Orange Slice, for garnish*

PREPARATION:

Fill your shaker with crushed ice. Add all five ingredients. Shake the mix vigorously for about thirty seconds. Strain over ice into a tall glass. Garnish with the Slice of Orange.

Starfish

After one sip, you'll be ready to lend everyone a hand.

INGREDIENTS:

1 jigger Light Rhum
½ jigger Orange Juice
4 dashes Grenadine
2 jiggers Tonic Water
Orange Slice, for garnish

PREPARATION:

Fill a rocks glass with ice. Pour in the Rhum, the Juice, the Grenadine, and the Tonic Water. Stir once or twice. Garnish with the Slice of Orange.

Survivor

After one sip, you'll be okay through the thick and the thin.

INGREDIENTS:

2 jiggers Rhum
1 t. sugar
Juice of ½ Lemon
Club Soda
Lemon Wedge, for garnish

PREPARATION:

Spoon the Sugar into a rocks glass, then fill with ice. Add the Rhum amd Juice, then top with Club Soda. Swizzle. Garnish with the Wedge of Lemon

SWAMP WATER

After one sip, you'll crawl on yer belly like a gator.

INGREDIENTS:

> *1 jigger Rhum*
> *½ jigger Orange Juice*
> *½ jigger Lemon Juice*
> *3 dashes Blue Curaçao*
> *Orange Peel, for garnish*

PREPARATION:

> Fill a rocks glass with ice. Pour in the Rhum, Juices, and the Curaçao. Stir once or twice. Garnish with the Twist of Orange.

SWIMMING ASHORE (FOR THE SONGS OF SUNRISE)

After one sip, you'll be washed up before long.

INGREDIENTS:

> *1 jigger Light Rhum*
> *½ jigger Cointreau*
> *2 jiggers Grapefruit Juice*
> *½ jigger Orange Juice*
> *½ jigger Grenadine*
> *Orange Slice, for garnish*

PREPARATION:

> Fill your shaker with crushed ice. Add the Rhum, Cointreau, Juices, and the Grenadine. Shake the mix vigorously for thirty seconds. Strain over ice into a rocks glass. Garnish with the Slice of Orange.

- T -

Talking Statue

After one sip, your lips will move like plaster.

Ingredients:
1 jigger Gin
Juice of 1 Lime
2 dashes Crème de Menthe
Dash Bitters
Cherry, for garnish

Preparation:
Fill your bar glass with ice. Add the Gin, Juice and Crème de Menthe. Stir thoroughly. Strain into a chiiled cocktail glass. Garnish with the Cherry.

Tampico Trauma

After one sip, they won't want to see you 'round here again.

Ingredients:
1 jigger Tequila
½ jigger 151 Rhum
½ jigger Amaretto.
Lime Wedge, for garnish

PREPARATION:

Fill your bar glass with ice. Add the Tequila, the 151 Rhum, and the Amaretto. Stir thoroughly. Strain over ice into a collins glass. Garnish with the Wedge of Lime.

TEQUILA MOONRISE

After one sip, you'll swear you'll never drink it again.

INGREDIENTS:

1 jigger Tequila
½ jigger Light Rhum
½ jigger Dark Rhum
Juice of ½ Lime
Juice of ½ Lemon
1 t. Superfine Sugar
1½ jiggers Ale

PREPARATION:

Spoon the Sugar into your shaker, then fill with crushed ice. Add the Tequila, Rhums, and Juices. Shake the mix vigorously for about thirty seconds. Strain over ice into a collins glass. Top with Ale.

TEQUILA SUNRISE

After one sip, you'll fly like an eagle.

INGREDIENTS:

1 jigger Tequila
2 jiggers Orange Juice
½ jigger Grenadine
Orange Slice, for garnish

PREPARATION:

Fill your shaker with crushed ice. Add the Tequila and Orange Juice. Shake the mix, then strain over ice into collins glass. To ensure that the Grenadine flows directly to the bottom for the "sunrise" effect, tilt the glass and pour the Grenadine directly down the inside. Do not stir. Garnish with the Slice of Orange.

Tequila Sunset

After one sip, you'll know you're not on Mallory Dock.

Ingredients:

> 1 jigger Tequila
> 1½ jiggers Orange Juice
> 1½ jiggers Pineapple Juice
> 1 T. Sugar, for rimming
> Slice of Orange, for garnish

Preparation:

Fill your blender one-quarter with crushed ice. Add the Tequila and Juices. Sugar the rim of a frosted cocktail glass. Blend on medium for thirty seconds, then pour into the frosted cocktail glass. Garnish with the Slice of Orange.

Texas Fizz

After one sip, you'll feel that nothing's changed at all.

Ingredients:

> 1 jigger Gin
> Juice of ¼ Orange
> Juice of ¼ Lemon
> Dash Grenadine
> Champagne, chilled
> Slice of Orange, for garnish

Preparation:

Fill your shaker with crushed ice. Add the Gin, Juices, and Grenadine. Shake the mix thoroughly. Strain over ice into a rocks glass. Fill with champagne. Garnish with the Slice of Orange.

TIA MARIA CULPA

After one sip, you won't give a damn who's at fault.

INGREDIENTS:

½ jigger Tia Maria
½ jigger Kahlúa
½ jigger Irish Cream

PREPARATION:

Fill your shaker with crushed ice. Add the Tia Maria, Kahlúa, and Irish Cream. Shake the mix vigorously for about thirty seconds. Strain into a chilled cocktail glass.

TIRE SWING

After one sip, you'll feel you're at the end of your rope.

1 jigger Amaretto
2 jiggers Dark Rhum
Juice of 2 Oranges
Slice of Orange, for garnish

PREPARATION:

Fill your bar glass with crushed ice. Add the Amaretto, Rhum, and Juice. Stir thoroughly, then strain over ice into a rocks glass. Garnish with the Slice of Orange.

TRAVIS MCGEE

After one sip, you'll believe anything John McDonald says.

INGREDIENTS:

1 jigger Rhum
½ t. Powdered Sugar
Juice of 1 Lime
½ oz. Grenadine
Lime Slice, for garnish

PREPARATION:

Spoon the Sugar into your shaker, then fill with crushed ice. Add the Tequila, Juice, and Grenadine. Shake the mix vigorously for about thirty seconds. Strain over ice into a sour glass. Garnish with the Slice of Lime.

TREETOP FLYER

After one sip, you'll be runnin' low and fast.

INGREDIENTS:

1 jigger Dry Gin
½ jigger Lemon Juice
2 t. Maraschino Liqueur
Lemon Peel, for garnish

PREPARATION:

Fill your shaker with ice. Add the Gin, the Juice, and the Maraschino. Shake the mix vigorously for about thirty seconds. Strain into a chilled cocktail glass. Garnish with the Twist of Lemon.

TRINIDAD

After one sip, you'll want to go home.

INGREDIENTS:

1 jigger Rhum
Juice of ½ Lime
1 t. Powdered Sugar
3 dashes Bitters
Lime Peel, for garnish

PREPARATION:

Spoon the Sugar into your shaker, then fill with crushed ice. Add the Rhum, Juice, and Bitters. Shake the mix vigorously for about thirty seconds. Strain into a chilled cocktail glass. Garnish with the Twist of Lime.

TRIP AROUND THE SUN

After one sip, you'll learn to just enjoy this ride.

INGREDIENTS:
1½ jiggers Rye Whiskey
½ jigger Maraschino Liqueur
½ jigger Lemon Juice
Lemon Peel, for garnish

PREPARATION:
Fill your shaker with ice. Add the Rye, Maraschino, and Juice. Shake the mix vigorously. Strain into a chilled cocktail glass. Garnish with the Twist of Lemon.

TROPICAL RAINSTORM

After one sip, you'll hear the sound of Heaven's ragtime band.

INGREDIENTS:
1 jigger Dark Rhum
½ jigger Cherry Brandy
Juice of ½ Lemon
1 t. Cointreau
Orange Peel, for garnish

PREPARATION:
Fill your shaker with crushed ice. Add the Rhum, Brandy, Juice, and Cointreau. Shake the mix vigorously. Strain into chilled cocktail glass. Garnish with the Twist of Orange.

TWELVE VOLT MAN

After one sip, you'll have sparks flyin' 'round your head.

INGREDIENTS:
2 jiggers Tequila
1 jigger Sambuca
6 Coffee Beans

PREPARATION:

Fill your blender one-quarter with ice. Add the Tequila, Sambuca, and Coffee Beans. Blend on low about one minute or until smooth. Pour into a chilled cocktail glass.

TWENTY THOUSAND LEAGUES

After one sip, you'll be changing channels.

INGREDIENTS:

1 jigger Gin
½ jigger Dry Vermouth
1 t. Pernod
2 dashes Orange Bitters
Orange Peel, for garnish

PREPARATION:

Fill your shaker with ice. Add the Gin, Vermouth, Pernod, and Bitters. Shake the mix vigorously for about thirty seconds. Strain into a chilled cocktail glass. Garnish with the Twist of Orange.

- U, V, W, X, Y & Z -

UNPOPULAR POET

After one sip, you'll be fresh out of rhymes.

INGREDIENTS:
1 jigger Blackberry Brandy
½ jigger Port
½ jigger Brandy
Orange Peel, for garnish

PREPARATION:
Fill your shaker with ice. Add the Port and both Brandies. Shake the mix vigorously for about thirty seconds. Strain into a chilled cocktail glass. Garnish with the Twist of Orange.

VAMPIRE'S MUMMY

After one sip, your ears will dong, then they'll ding.

INGREDIENTS:
1 jigger Scotch
¾ jigger Cherry Brandy
¾ jigger Sweet Vermouth
¾ jigger Orange Juice
Orange Slice, for garnish

PREPARATION:

Fill your shaker with ice. Add in the Scotch, Brandy, Vermouth, and Juice. Shake the mix vigorously for about thirty seconds. Strain into a chilled cocktail glass. Garnish with the Slice of Orange.

VOLCANO

After one sip, you just won't know where you're a-gonna go.

INGREDIENTS:

1 jigger Vodka
1 jigger Cinnamon Schnapps
Dash Tabasco

PREPARATION:

Fill your shaker with ice. Add the Vodka and Schnapps. Shake the mix vigorously for about thirty seconds. Strain into a tall shot glass. Add Tabasco. Savor, rather than shoot,

WATERSPOUT

After one sip, you'll be spewing a lot of stuff.

INGREDIENTS:

1 jigger Gold Tequila
½ jigger Crème de Cacao
½ jigger Sweet Cream
Whipped Cream
Powdered Cocoa

PREPARATION:

Fill your bar glass with cracked ice. Add the Tequila, Crème de Cacao, and Sweet Cream. Shake the mixture vigorously until it begins to foam. Strain into a chilled cocktail glass. Top with a dollop of Whipped Cream. Dust with the Powdered Cocoa.

WILDE OSCAR

After one sip, you'd better stay out of bed.

INGREDIENTS:
>   *1 jigger Brandy*
>   *½ jigger Sweet Vermouth*
>   *1 t. Lemon Juice*
>   *1 t. Simple Syrup**
>   *Lemon Peel, for garnish*
>
>   ** A recipe for preparing a Simple Syrup can be found in the Glossary.*

PREPARATION:
> Fill your shaker with shaved ice. Add in the Brandy, Vermouth, Juice, and the Simple Syrup. Shake the mix vigorously for about thirty seconds. Strain into a chilled cocktail glass. Garnish with the Twist of Lemon.

WILD MERIDIAN

After one sip, you'll never be able to cross back.

INGREDIENTS:
>   *2 jiggers Holland Gin*
>   *1 jigger Dry Vermouth*
>   *2 dashes Simple Syrup**
>   *2 dashes Peychaud's Bitters*
>   *Dash Pernod*
>   *Lemon Peel, for garnish*
>
>   ** A recipe for preparing a Simple Syrup can be found in the Glossary.*

PREPARATION:
> Fill your shaker with shaved ice. Add the Gin, Vermouth, Bitters, Pernod, and Simple Syrup. Shake the mixture vigorously for about thirty seconds. Strain into a chilled cocktail glass. Garnish with the Twist of Lemon.

XAVIER'S DANCE

After one sip, you'll shuffle across the floor just like Cugey.

INGREDIENTS:

1 jigger Tequila
½ jigger White Crème de Cacao
½ jigger Simple Syrup*
1 jigger Cream

* A recipe for preparing a Simple Syrup can be found in the Glossary.

PREPARATION:

Fill your blender one-quarter with ice. Add in all the ingredients. Blend on medium about one minute or until smooth. Pour into a chilled cocktail glass.

X MARKS THE SPOT

After one sip, your eyes will cross and you'll see spots.

INGREDIENTS:

1 jigger Light Rhum
½ jigger Triple Sec
Juice of ½ Lemon
Orange Peel, for garnish

PREPARATION:

Fill your shaker with shaved ice. Add the Rhum, Triple Sec, and Juice. Shake the mix vigorously for about thirty seconds. Strain into a chilled cocktail glass. Garnish with the Twist of Orange.

YELLOW BIRD

After one sip, you won't be chicken anymore.

INGREDIENTS:

1 jigger Rhum

½ jigger Galliano
½ jigger Crème de Banana
1½ jiggers Orange Juice
1 jigger Pineapple Juice
Orange Slice, for garnish

PREPARATION:
Fill your shaker with shaved ice. Add all the ingredients.
Shake the mixture vigorously. Strain over ice into a rocks
glass. Garnish with the Slice of Orange.

YELLOW PARROT

After one sip, you won't have an original thing to say.

INGREDIENTS:
1 jigger Apricot Brandy
1 jigger Yellow Chartreuse
1 jigger Pernod
Cherry, for garnish

PREPARATION:
Fill your shaker with shaved ice. Add the Brandy, Yellow
Chartreuse, and Pernod. Shake the mixture vigorously for
thirty seconds. Strain into a chilled cocktail glass. Garnish
with the Cherry.

Yo Ho Ho

After one sip, you'll treasure the rest of the drink.

INGREDIENTS:
1 jigger Rhum
1 jigger Swedish Punsch
1 jigger Calvados
Lemon Peel, for garnish

PREPARATION:
Fill your shaker with ice. Add the Rhum, Swedish Punsch,

and Calvados. Shake the mixture vigorously for thirty seconds. Strain into a chilled cocktail glass. Garnish with the Twist of Lemon.

ZOMBIE

After one sip, you'll feel like an MTV host.

INGREDIENTS:

½ jigger Rhum
½ jigger Dark Rhum
½ jigger Apricot Brandy
1 jigger Pineapple Juice
1 jigger Sour Mix*
¼ jigger 151 Rhum

A recipe for preparing a Sour Mix can be found in the Glossary.

PREPARATION:

Fill your shaker with crushed ice. Add in the Rhums, Brandy, Juice, and Sour Mix. Shake the mix vigorously for about thirty seconds. Strain over ice into a rocks glass. Float the 151 Rhum on top.

Roll with the Punches

BARBADOS BOWL

After one sip, you'll want to put on your best muu-muu.

INGREDIENTS:
> *1 pt. Light Rhum*
> *1 pt. Dark Rhum*
> *3 pts. Pineapple Juice*
> *1 pt. Mango Nectar*
> *8 Bananas*
> *1 cup Sugar*
> *Juice of 8 Limes*
> *1 Block of Ice*
> *2 Limes, sliced for garnish*

PREPARATION:
> Slice six of the Bananas into your blender. Add the Sugar
> and the Lime Juice. Blend on medium at least one minute
> until smooth. Pour the mix into a punch bowl. Add the
> Rhums, Pineapple Juice, and Mango Nectar. Add the Ice.
> Slice the remaining two Bananas and float with the Slices
> of Lime on top of the punch.

CARMEN'S HEADGEAR PUNCH

After one sip, you won't dance like this anymore.

INGREDIENTS:

1 lb. Brown Sugar
2 qts. Orange Juice
Juice of 6 Lemons
5 Bananas, sliced
1 fresh Pineapple, cut in pieces
4 qts. White Wine
2 qts. Light Rhum
1 qt. Jamaican Rhum
1 qt. Crème de Banana
1 Block of Ice

INGREDIENTS:

In a large crock, combine the Fruit (with their rinds), the Juices, the Sugar, and the Wine. Stir thoroughly, cover, and allow the mixture to set overnight in a cool place.

The next morning, add the Rhums and the Crème de Banana. Strain into a punch bowl. Add the Ice.

COSMIC PUNCH

After one sip, you'll hear universal laughter among the stars.

INGREDIENTS:

¾ pt. Light Rhum
½ pt. Dark Rhum
½ pt. Peppermint Schnapps
1 qt. Mango Nectar
1 pt. Cream
1 qt. Orange Juice
6 Mint Sprigs
1 Fresh Mango, cut in pieces
1 Orange, sliced
1 Block of Ice

PREPARATION:

In large punch bowl, combine the Rhums, Schnapps, Mango Nectar, and Cream. Stir thoroughly. Add Ice. Float the Sprigs of Mint, the Pieces of Mango, and the Slices of Orange. Refrigerate at least an hour.

DON' CHU KNOW PUNCH

After one sip, you'll know how long you can go.

INGREDIENTS:

8 oz. Orange Juice concentrate
1 qt. Light Rhum
2 cups Crushed Ice
1 T. Vanilla Extract
2 qts. Cream Soda

PREPARATION:

Blend together the Orange concentrate, Rhum, and Ice. Place the mixture in the freezer until the mix becomes a slush. Add Ice to a punch bowl, then mix in the slush. Add the Cream Soda slowly to minimize the loss of carbonation. Stir only once or twice.

FISH HOUSE PUNCH (No. 1)

After one sip, you'll stand around with baited breath.

INGREDIENTS:

¾ lb. Sugar
1 qt. Lemon Juice
2 qts. Jamaican Rhum
2 qts. Water
Peach Brandy, to taste
1 Block of Ice

PREPARATION:

In large punch bowl, dissolve the Sugar with a little of

the Water. Stir in the Lemon Juice, Rhum, and remaining Water. Add Peach Brandy, to taste. Place the Ice in the punch bowl. Allow to chill for two hours.

FISH HOUSE PUNCH (No. 2)

After one sip, baited breath is better than no breath at all!

INGREDIENTS:

> 1½ cups Sugar
> 1 cup Water
> 3 cups Lemon Juice
> 1 qt. Dry White Wine
> 1 qt.. Jamaica Rhum
> 1 qt. Gold Label Rhum
> 1 qt. Cognac
> 2½ jiggers Peach Brandy
> 1 Block of Ice

PREPARATION:

In large punch bowl, dissolve the Sugar with the Water and Lemon Juice. Stir in the Wine, Rhums, Cognac, and Brandy. Allow this to stand two hours, stirring now and then. Before serving, add the Ice and stir to cool.

FLAMINGO PUNCH

After one sip, you'll be giving everyone else the bird.

INGREDIENTS:

> 1 qt. Champagne
> 1 qt. Crackling Rosé Wine
> 1 pt. frozen Whole Raspberries, thawed
> 1 Block of Ice

PREPARATION:

In large punch bowl, place the block of ice along with the Raspberries. Stir in the Champagne and Wine.

HURRICANE SEASON PUNCH

After one sip, you won't run at this pace very long.

INGREDIENTS:
> 1 qt. *Southern Comfort*
> 8 oz. *Orange Juice concentrate*
> 8 oz. *Lemonade concentrate*
> ¼ cup *Lemon Juice*
> 2 qts. *7-Up*
> 1 *Block of Ice*

PREPARATION:
> In large punch bowl, combine the Southern Comfort and Juices. Just before serving, add the Ice, then the 7-Up.

MARINA PUNCH

After one sip, you'll think your ringing ears are a call from Steve Martin asking if you want to "get small."

INGREDIENTS:
> 2 qts. *Rhum*
> 8 oz. *Orange Juice concentrate*
> 8 oz. *Lemonade concentrate*
> 8 oz. *Pineapple Juice concentrate*
> 8 oz. *Simple Syrup**
> *Assorted Tropical Fruits*
> 1 *Block of Ice*
>
> * *A recipe for preparing a Simple Syrup can be found in the Glossary.*

PREPARATION:
> Set the block of Ice in a punch bowl. Pour all ingredients over the Ice. Stir in the Fruits. Allow to chill at least one hour.

Navy Punch

After one sip, you'll have both hands on deck.

Ingredients:
4 fresh Pineapples, sliced
1 lb. fine granulated Sugar
1 pt. Dark Rhum
1 pt. Cognac
1 pt. Peach Brandy
Juice of 4 Lemons
4 qts. Champagne, chilled
1 Block of Ice
Fresh fruits, for garnish

Preparation:
In a large punch bowl, sprinkle the sliced Pineapples with Sugar. Allow the Sugar to dissolve. Add in the Rhum, Cognac, Brandy, and Lemon juice. Stir well. Add the Ice. Slowly add the chilled Champagne. Garnish with the Fresh Fruits.

Rhum Punch

After one sip, you'll learn to roll with the punches.

Ingredients:
½ pt. Puerto Rican Rhum
½ pt. Peach Brandy
1 cup Lime Juice
5 T. Bitters
2 qts. Soda Water
1 Block of Ice

Preparation:
In large punch bowl, combine the Rhum, Brandy, Lime Juice, and Bitters. Just before serving, add the Ice, then stir in the Soda Water.

TAHITIAN PUNCH

After one sip, you'll know you don't drink this often enough.

INGREDIENTS:

1 pt. Light Rhum
1 pt. Dark Rhum
½ pt. Cream of Coconut
½ pt. Sloe Gin
4 oz. Peppermint Schnapps
1 oz. Grenadine
3 pts. Unsweetened Pineapple Juice
4 oz. Lime Juice
4 oz. Club Soda
1 Pineapple, sliced for garnish
1 Orange, sliced for garnish
1 Block of Ice

PREPARATION:

In large punch bowl, combine the Rhums, Cream of Coconut, Sloe Gin, Schnapps, and Grenadine. Stir well. Add the Ice and Garnish. Refrigerate at least one hour. Add Club Soda just before serving.

Temperance Zone

BAD HANDSTAND

After one sip, you'll know some of the answers.

INGREDIENTS:
> Complete peel of 1 Lemon
> Ginger Ale

PREPARATION:
> In an unbroken spiral, carefully peel the rind from a Lemon. Place the peel in a collins glass with one end of the rind hooked over rim. Add ice, then fill with Ginger Ale.

BLOODY SHAME

After one sip, you'll be able to stand up and focus.

INGREDIENTS:
> ½ cup Tomato Juice
> 1 jigger Heinz 57
> Juice of ½ Lemon
> ¼ t. Garlic Salt
> 2 dashes Worcestershire
> 1 dash Tabasco
> Black Pepper, freshly ground
> Large Shrimp, peeled & deveined (tail on)
> Lemon Wedge, fot garnish

PREPARATION:

Fill your shaker with cracked ice. Add the first seven ingredients. Shake the mix vigorously for about thirty seconds. Strain over ice into a rocks glass. Garnish with the Shrimp and the Wedge of Lemon.

CALYPSO POET

After one sip, you'll have had your fun.

INGREDIENTS:

2 T. Lemon Juice
½ t. Superfine Sugar
2 dashes Angostura Bitters
Ginger Beer
Lemon Slice, for garnish

PREPARATION:

Place ice cubes in a collins glass. Add only the first three ingredients. Stir well. Add Ginger Beer. Garnish with the Slice of Lemon.

LITTLE MISS MAGIC

After one sip, you'll catch a little dialogue coming your way.

INGREDIENTS:

3 T. Lime Juice
½ jigger Raspberry Syrup
Club Soda
Lime Wedge, for garnish

PREPARATION:

Place ice cubes in a collins glass. Add Lime Juice and Syrup. Stir well, but gently. Add Club Soda, then swizzle. Garnish with the Wedge of Lime.

LOVELY LADY

After one sip, you'll enjoy a little quiet and comfort.

INGREDIENTS:

> *Juice of 1 Orange*
> *1 jigger Cranberry Juice*
> *Fresca*
> *Orange Slice, for garnish*

PREPARATION:

> Place ice cubes in a collins glass. Add the Juices and stir once or twice. Add the Fresca and swizzle. Garnish with the Slice of Orange.

NAUGHTY MARGARITA

After one sip, you'll like it, but you'll know it's not a real . . .

INGREDIENTS:

> *½ cup Lime concentrate*
> *½ cup Orange Juice*
> *½ cup Grapefruit Juice (unsweetened)*
> *10-15 Ice Cubes*
> *Lime Wedge, for garnish*
> *Coarse Sugar or Salt*

PREPARATION:

> First, sugar or salt the rim of a rocks glass by placing coarse sugar or salt on a saucer, rubbing the rim of the glass with with the Lime, then dipping the rim into the sugar or salt for a thorough coating.
>
> Add the Juices to your blender. Cover and blend low until smooth. As the blender hums away, drop one ice cube at a time through the hole in the cover until this becomes a slushy concoction. Pour into the glass. Garnish with the Wedge of Lime.

PARENTAL WARNING

After one sip, you'll be ready to shake it up, baby.

INGREDIENTS:

2 T. Lemon Juice
1 T. Grenadine
Club Soda
Lemon Slice, for garnish

PREPARATION:

Place ice cubes in a collins glass. Add the Lemon Juice and Grenadine. Stir thoroughly. Top off with Club Soda. Swizzle. Garnish with the Slice of Lemon.

Glossary

A

ABISANTE: Liqueur with anise (licorice) flavor.

ABSINTHE: Illegal for years in the U.S., this redistilled alcohol containing wormwood is once again available on the American market. *See* VERMOUTH.

ADVOKAAT: Liqueur with eggnog flavor. (Holland)

AKVAVIT: Produced from rye and infused with caraway. (Scandinavia)

AMARETTO: Liqueur with almond flavor, but produced from apricot pits. (Italy)

AMERICAN WHISKEY: When produced in the United States, this RYE WHISKEY must be made from a mash of at least 51 percent rye, the remainder of which can be corn and/or malted barley. Distilled to not more than 160 (U.S.) proof, the whiskey must be diluted to not more than 125 (U.S.) proof, then aged in charred, new oak barrels. Any such whiskey aged for two years or more is termed "straight rye whiskey." Jim Beam and Wild Turkey are among the most popular brands.

AMER PICON: APÉRITIF produced from oranges, quinine and gentian. (France)

ANGOSTURA: *See* Bitters

ANISETTE: Liqueur with licorice flavor produced from anise seed.

APÉRITIF: Light, alcoholic drink served before a meal; one of a variety of wines or bitters.

APPLE BRANDY: Liqueur with apple flavor; applejack.

APRICOT LIQUEUR: Cordial produced from apricot pits.

ARMAGNAC: Like cognac, a quality brandy distilled only once and in vintages.

B

BANANA LIQUEUR: See CRÈME DE BANANA

BAR GLASS: Often used also as a BEER GLASS, this glass with a capacity of 16 ounces is often used for mixing drinks which require either stirring with ice or shaking (with visibility of the contents) before being strained into the serving glass. Also, MIXING GLASS.

BENEDICTINE: Liqueur produced from secret formula of herbs by monks of the Benedictine order. (France)

BITTERS: APÉRITIF with sweet flavor produced from aromatic plants mixed with alcohol or glycerine.

BLACKBERRY LIQUEUR: Cordial produced from blackberries.

BOURBON: Recognized as "America's favorite whiskey," this liquor is produced from a combination of grains, at least 51% of which must be corn. Like AMERICAN RYE WHISKEY, this is a *straight* whiskey that must be aged in casks of charred, white oak for no less than 2 years. It is bottled in proofs ranging from 80 to 125.

Sometimes called "Dixie Nectar," this was originally known in Bourbon County, Virginia (which now belongs to Kentucky) as "corn whiskey." By the mid-1800s, it was so closely associated with its region that folks simply called it "bourbon," or "Kentucky bourbon."

BRANDY: The French have a phrase for this liquor: *eau de vie,* "water of life." Quite different from the Scandinavian concept of "water of life" AKVAVIT, this distillate comes from one or more wines or fermented fruit juices, and may be colored with caramel.

Despite the French and Scandinavian phrases, though, the name comes from the Dutch word *brandewijn,* which means "to burn" or "to distill." Language aside, the best of the lot is still produced wholly of grapes from the Grande Champagne area in the Cognac region of France; hence, *cognac.*

Beyond France, brandies of high character are produced in Germany, Spain, and Portugal. The muscat grapes of Greece give us deep, rich METAXA, while Peru sends us PISCO.

Understand that many ingredients in this glossary are brandies: distilled wines of their respective fruits.

C

CANADIAN WHISKY: Unlike AMERICAN WHISKEY, this is no "straight" whiskey produced in Canada. All legal whisky [note the spelling] made north of the border is a blend of multi-grains (generally corn and rye), but there is no requirement that rye must be included. Still, as long as the spirits "possess the aroma, taste and character generally attributed to Canadian whisky," their bottles can be labeled as "Canadian Whisky," "Canadian Rye Whisky," or "Rye Whisky." The other distinction is that whisky must be aged for at least three years in a small, wooden barrel with a capacity no larger than 700 liters.

CAMPARI: Bitter APÉRITIF with astringent, bittersweet flavor used as either an ingredient, or by itself on-the-rocks. Also in a sweet variety. (Italy)

CHAMBORD: Liqueur produced from small black raspberries. (France)

CHAMBRAISE: Liqueur made from wild strawberries. (France)

CHARTREUSE: Liqueur (yellow or green) produced from a secret formula of herbs by monks of the Carthusian order. (France)

CHERRY: Variety of small, red berries used as flavorings and in producing CORDIALS and BRANDIES.

The Greek word *kerasos* became *chery* in Middle English.

Originating in Asia, the fruit was spread widely across Europe and North America in prehistoric times. Colonists in the New World found cherries growing wild and crossbred them with varieties from the Old World.

Italy's *marasca* cherry is the one used in the CORDIAL called MARASCHINO or

MARASCHINE. In turn, this is the flavoring for a preserved cherry called MARASCHINO CHERRY, which is used as a garnish in several drinks.

CHERRY HEERING: Liqueur produced from cherries. (Denmark)

CHERRY MARNIER: Liqueur produced from cherries and almonds. (France)

CLARET: Red table wine of the Bordeaux region of France.

CLUB SODA: Nothing more than flavorless water given a high charge of carbonic acid gas, this is the basis of a great many drinks, with or without alcohol. If nothing, it lends sparkle and fizz to an otherwise dull container.

COCKTAIL GLASS: More or less a generic term for any broad-mouthed stemware with a capacity of 4 or 5 ounces. The stem is key, for it allows a cold drink without ice to be held apart from the body heat of the drinker's hand. Also, MARTINI GLASS.

COCONUT: The coconut palm (*Cocos nucifera*) yields these hard-shelled pods that hold a white meat and a milky liquid.

Known in Egypt as early as the 6th century and seen by Marco Polo in the Far East and India, coconuts were also found along the Pacific shores of Hawaii and South America. Still its origins are unknown, and many believe that pods drifted across the Pacific from the plant's native soil of tropical America

COCONUT MILK: This is not simply the liquid from the coconut, which is known as *coconut water.*

Nor is this the same as CREAM OF COCONUT, a thicker processed liquid introduced in the 1950s.

To make Coconut Milk:
   3 cups Milk, from a cow!
   3 cups fresh Coconut Meat, grated coarse

In a saucepan, combine the Milk and grated Coconut.

Simmer over low heat until foam forms on surface.

Strain and chill.

COFFEE LIQUEUR: Liqueur produced from coffee beans.

COGNAC: Brandy of top quality, distilled only once, from this region of France.

COINTREAU: Liqueur of top quality produced from skins of green CURAÇAO oranges in the Caribbean. First mentioned in print in 1813, CURAÇAO recipes had been listed in cookbooks of the early 19th century. See CURAÇAO, TRIPLE SEC

COLA: A carbonated soft drink made from the kola nut, a brownish seed (about the size of a chestnut) from the *Cola nitida* tree that grows in tropical Africa, the West Indies, and Brazil. The kola nut contains caffeine as well as theobromine, both stimulants.

COLLINS, TOM: Tall mixed drink containing SOUR MIX, CLUB SODA, and liquor (GIN or VODKA). When made with WHISK(E)Y, this becomes a FRED COLLINS.

COLLINS GLASS: A tall glass with a capacity of 10 to 12 ounces, which will hold about 8 ounces of spirit mixed with juice plus ice. Also, HIGHBALL GLASS.

COOLER: Mixed drink containing a carbonated mixer with a spirit or a wine.

CORDIAL: Also LIQUEUR.

CRÈME DE BANANA: Liqueur with a sweet banana flavor.

CURAÇAO: Generic name for liqueur produced from skins of CURAÇAO oranges. See COINTREAU, TRIPLE SEC

This recipe for "curacoa" appeared in 1857 in *Mrs. Hale's New Cook Book* by Sarah J. Hale.

   1 lb. of the dried peel of Seville oranges

8 pt. Brandy
2 pt. Water
5 lbs. Sugar
3 pt. Water

Wash the Peel in lukewarm water.
Put Peel in jars. Add Brandy and Water.
Let stand for 2 weeks, shaking often.
Melt Sugar in Water. Mix with liquour.
Strain.

CRANBERRY LIQUEUR: Liqueur produced from cranberries.

CREAM OF COCONUT: See COCONUT MILK.

CRÈME LIQUEUR: Any of a number of liqueurs with a creamy consistency produced by a high sugar content.

CRÈME DE ANANAS: Liqueur produced from pineapples.

CRÈME DE BANANA: Liqueur produced from bananas.

CRÈME DE CACAO: Liqueur (white or dark) produced from cacao beans.

CRÈME DE CASSIS: Liquer produced from black currants.

CRÈME DE MENTHE: Liqueur (white or green) produced from mint.

CRÈME DE NOYAUX: Almond-flavored, pink liqueur made from apricot pits. French variation of the Italian liqueur AMARETTO.

CRÈME DE PAMPLEMOUSSE: Sweet liqueur made from the natural extracts of pink grapefruit.

CRÈME DE VANILLE: Liquer produced from vanilla beans, a part of an orchid.

CURAÇAO: Liqueur (orange or blue) produced from skins of the CURAÇAO orange. *See* COINTREAU, TRIPLE SEC

D

DRAMBUIE: Liqueur produced from Scotch malt whiskey.

DUBONNET: Bittersweet, fortified wine-based APÉRITIF flavored with herbs and quinine. (France)

F

FALERNUM: Sweetener produced from LIMES and spices. Rarely available these days, this once served as a key ingredient in the tiki-cocktails of the mid-20th century.

To make Falrnum:
  Peels from 10 Limes,
  10 Whole Cloves
  5 Whole Almonds, unsalted
  1 t. Sugar
  1 liter White Rhum

Use a vegetable peeler to remove the green, top layer from the limes. Be certain to remove any white pith inside the peels.

Reserve the lime sections for some other use, or squeeze them for their juices.

In a large glass container, combine the Peels, Cloves, Unsalted Almonds, and Sugar with the White Rhum.

Cover loosely, then store for three days in a sunny place.

Carefully strain the mixture into another clean, glass container. Discard the solids.

Cover tightly and store at room temperature.

FIX: Sour drink made with PINEAPPLE syrup and ice.

FIZZ: Tall mixed drink of SOUR MIX, sugar, CLUB SODA, and liquor; may also include egg white.

FRAISES: Liqueur produced from strawberries, high sugar content.

FRAISES DE BOIS: From France, "wild strawberries."

FRAMBOISE: Liqueur produced from raspberries, high alcohol content.

FRANGELICO: Liqueur produced from hazelnuts. (Italy)

G

GALLIANO: Liqueur (gold) produced from spices and herbs. (Italy)

GIN: Originally concocted in Holland for medicinal purposes during the 17th century, this distilled spirit produced from grain alcohol first created by Franz de le Boë (1614-1672), a professor at the University of Leiden is flavored with juniper berries (as well as other berries, seeds, herbs, and roots). The name comes from the Dutch word for "juniper," *genever*.

Unlike WHISKEY, which is often drunk straight or on-the-rocks, this is most often used in a mixed drink. The exception, though, remains for true Dutch (HOLLAND) gin, which is best straight. Outside of Holland, though, many distillers have added distinctive flavors from coriander, orange peels, or cardamom. In Britain, these include LONDON DRY gin, as well as PLYMOUTH gin. The latter lacks the bitter botanicals of London Dry.

Because of the simplicity of the recipe and the distilling process, gin remains one of the easiest liquors to make. While it might have been made privately most often during the Prohibition Era, it remains the product of back-country stills, where it is better known simply as "white lightning."

GINGER BEER: Like root beer, birch beer, or even ginger ale, this is a non-alcoholic beverage. Flavored with fermented ginger, it was first popular in the United Kingdom in the early 19th century. In America, it became appreciated as a substitute for "real" beer.

To make Ginger Beer:

2 oz. Ginger Root, pounded
½ cup Lemon Juice
1 lb. Sugar
4 qts. Water
1 oz. yeast

Mix the pounded Ginger Root, the Lemon Juice, and the Sugar in a large crock fitted with a cover.

Add boiling Water and mix.

Dissolve Yeast in a small amount of water. When the main concoction has cooled to 110° F., add dissolved yeast and stir.

Cover and allow to ferment for 1 week. Strain into bottles. Makes 1 gallon.

GOBLET: Round stemware with a capacity of 8 to 10 ounces, which will hold about 7 ounces of beverage without ice.

GRAND MARNIER: Liqueur with cognac base and orange flavor. (France)

GRAPEFRUIT: Yellow, globular citrus fruit that grows in grape-like clusters on a tropical tree. Sometimes called "pomelo," because it is confused with the true pomelo tree, whose seeds were brought from Indonesia to the island of Barbados by Capt. Shaddock in 1896. The grapefruit might well be a mutation of that plant.

Odette Philippe, a French count, brought the fruit to Tampa, Florida in 1823, but commercial plantings did not come until 1885. By 1900, the fruit had become a part of breakfast diets.

Today, more than half of the crop is marketed as juice.

GRENADINE: Sweet flavoring (red) produced from pomegranates.

H

HAVANA CLUB: Havana Club is "El Ron de Cuba" (The Rum of Cuba) produced in the national distillery. As of this writing, the U.S. still has its trade embargo against the island's government. So, this rum remains contraband with a capital C; however, the spirit is available in Mexico, Canada, and nations throughout the Caribbean. A recipe might come close with another fine, light rhum.

HIGHBALL: Tall drink combination of liquor (1½-2 oz.), mixer (juice or soda 6-10 oz.), and ice.

HIGHBALL GLASS: A tall glass with a capacity of 10 to 12 ounces, which will hold about 8 ounces of spirit mixed with a sparkling beverage plus ice. Also, COLLINS GLASS.

I

IRISH CREAM: Liqueur produced from Irish whiskey, cream, and sweetener.

IRISH MIST: Liqueur produced with Irish whiskey, oranges, and honey.

K

KAHLÚA: Liqueur of top quality produced from coffee beans. (Mexico)

KEY LIME: See LIME.

KIRSCH: Liqueur produced from black cherries; *kirschwasser.*

KÜMMEL: Liqueur with caraway flavor.

L

LEILANI RHUM: The Leilani spirit has not been produced for many years; however, every now and then a rare bottle might appear in the back of someone's forsaken bar or even the dusty, bottom shelf of some old liquor store. At one time, their magazine ads proclaimed: "An act of the gods made this the best-tasting rum in the world." And that might not have been far from the truth. Absent this rare spirit, a recipe might come close with another fine, white rhum.

LEMON: Tangy yellow citrus native to Asia, where the Persian word was *limun.*

Cultivated throughout the eastern Mediterranean for some 2500 years, the fruit was brought to Europe after the Crusades. While it is known that Spanish friars grew lemons in California, legend says that Columbus brought both lemon and lime seeds to Florida shores.

LICOR 43: A sweet, vanilla-flavored liqueur produced from some forty-three ingredients that include vanilla and fruits,

as well as aromatic herbs and spices. (Spain)

LILLET: APÉRITIF (white or red) made from wine, BRANDY, fruits, and herbs. (France)

LIME: Tangy, green citrus similar to a LEMON, whose origin is Southeast Asia, but whose name is from the Arabic *limah.*

Legend is that Columbus brought lime and LEMON seeds with him from Italy to Haiti in 1493. From there, the plant spread across the West Indies: west to Mexico; north to the Florida Keys.

After 1906, KEY LIME had become an important crop, but most groves were destroyed in a 1926 hurricane and replaced with a cross- breed of those grown in California. More yellow than the simple LIME, key limes are grown mostly on private, non-commercial lands in the Keys.

LIQUEUR: Sweetened syrupy spirit produced from fruits, peels, seeds, and herbs. The preferred term in England and France is CORDIAL, from the Medieval Latin, *cordialis,* and the Latin, *cor,* "heart."

Once used for medicinal purposes, the oldest cordial dates back to about 420 B.C. when Hippocrates concocted a mix of wine-sweetened honey and cinnamon. This tradition was carried on by several European orders of monks, many of whose own concoctions are now produced commercially.

There are three processes by which LIQUEURS (CORDIALS) are created. One is called *infusion* (*maceration*), in which flavorings are steeped in alcohol; another is called *percolation,* in which alcohol percolates above the flavorings; the third, *distillation,* in which the ingredients are distilled directly from their extracted flavors. Using copper pots, distillation produced colorless spirits of various proofs.

Fruit-flavored brandies are produced from a base of BRANDY; however, other kinds of LIQUEURS are produced from other spirits. See BRANDY.

LIQUOR: Alcoholic beverage which has been distilled, rather than fermented.

LOWBALL: See OLD FASHIONED

M

MANDARINE: Liqueur with cognac base and tangerine flavor.

MARASCHINO: Brandy produced from cherries and almonds.

MARASCHINO CHERRY: See CHERRY

METAXA: BRANDY. (Greece)

MIDORI: Liqueur with honeydew flavor. (Japan)

MILK BRANDY: See TUACA.

MIXING GLASS: Also, BAR GLASS.

O

ORANGE: A variety of round, yellow-red citrus originating in the Orient and cultivated in China as early as 2400 B.C. They were brought by the Moors in the 8th century to Spain, where the less bitter kind became known as "Seville oranges."

Columbus brought seeds from the Canary Islands to Hispaniola in 1493. Plantings by Spanish and Portuguese spread across the Carribbean, Mexico, and South America. Some credit Ponce de Leon with bringing them to Florida, but records indicate they were first planted in North America by Hernando de Soto in 1539 at St. Augustine. Spanish explorers later brought them from Mexico into California and Arizona.

After the United States acquired Florida in 1821, the crop became a profitable one. By the 1960s, the state and industry had its own national spokesperson in a former Miss America, Anita Bryant, chirping the official line: "A day without orange juice is like a day without sunshine."

ORANGE FLOWER WATER: Also called ORANGE BLOSSOM WATER

True hydrosols must be made by distilling the water in which the orange blossoms have been soaking; however, this recipe can provide an acceptable variation. For best results, use the flowers that are not blossoming on hybrids and pick the petals early in the morning, before the sun becomes too hot. Also, do not use flowers that have been sprayed with herbicides, pesticides, or insecticides.

To make Orange Flower Water:
    8 oz. Orange Flower Petals
    1 cup Water

Gently wash the petals in cool water and rinse them thoroughly.

Use a mortar & pestle made of stone or porcelain to break down the damp petals and allow them to release their oils. Allow this mix sit for four or five hours.

Into a large glass jar with a lid, add the orange petals and their juices, then add just enough distilled water to cover them. Do not add any more than a cup, because you can always add more later.

Loosely cover the jar with its lid and place it in a sunny location, where it should remain for at least two weeks.

After two weeks, uncover the jar and sample the scent. If the scent of orange is weak, let it remain in the sun another seven days.

Sterilize a small, lidded jar.

Strain orange water into sterilized jar.

Cover the orange water mix and store it in the refrigerator until needed.

ORGEAT: Orange and almond flavored syrup originally produced from barley in 18th-century England. The word, though is French, from the Latin *hordeum.*

To make Orgeat:
    1 Cinnamon stick
    ¼ lb. Almonds
    3 cups Milk
    1 cup Cream
    1 T. Rose Water *

Crush together Cinnamon and Almonds.
Add Milk, Cream, Rose Water.
Mix and sweeten to taste.
Boil, then strain.

* Rose Water can be made with the same process as ORANGE WATER.

P

PARFAIT AMOUR: Cordial produced from citron.

PASSION FRUIT LIQUEUR: Liqueur with mango or peach flavor. (Hawaii)

PEACH LIQUEUR: Liqueur with peach flavor.

PEAR LIQUEUR: Liqueur produced from pears. (Hungary)

PENAUT LOLITA: Liqueur produced from peanuts.

PEPPERMINT SCHNAPPS: Liqueur with light mint flavor.

PERNOD: Liqueur with licorice flavor.

PEYCHAUD'S: *See* Bitters

PINEAPPLE: Large ovular tropical fruit with spiny skin and swordlike leaves seen in Guadeloupe by Columbus, who called it *piña de Indes*, "pine of the Indians." The Indians of Paraguay and Brazil called a domesticated variety *naná*, or "excellent fruit." Magellan first exported the fruit to the Old World from Brazil in the 16th century, but it was also dispersed throughout the Asian tropics.

Captain James Cook took the fruit to Hawaii in 1790. And though it was also grown in Florida, there was no commercial market until the steamboat trade provided quick export in the 1880s.

PINEAPPLE LIQUEUR: Liqueur produced from pineapples.

POUSSE-CAFÉ: Different from mixed drink, a layered drink with each ingredient carefully floated atop the other, often in specific order.

POUSSE CAFÉ GLASS: Tall, narrow glass with either a heavy bottom or else a short stem, and with a capacity of 2 to 3 ounces, which will hold about 1.5 to 2 ounces of layered liqueurs for sipping.

PROOF: A number indicating alcoholic content, determined by doubling the percentage of alcohol (*e.g.*, an 80-proof spirit contains 40% alcohol).

PRUNELLE: Liqueur produced from meat, vanilla beans, figs, and plum pits.

PUNCH: Sometimes mixed in single servings, these are generally created in large bowls with various combinations of spirits, wines, fruits, sweeteners, and flavorings with juices or carbonated beverages.

Q

QUININE: Bitter, colorless powder from cinchona bark, also used to treat malaria.

R

ROCKS GLASS: A short, but wide, thick-bottomed glass with a capacity of 8 to 10 ounces, which will hold about 6 ounces of beverage plus ice. Generally, this is used for serving straight spirits over ice ("on the rocks"). Also, LOWBALL GLASS, OLD FASHIONED GLASS, SMALL GLASS.

ROSE'S LIME JUICE: Lime juice which has been both sweetened and concentrated. Now used as an ingredient for mixed drinks, this was concocted in 1867 by a Scotsman named Lauchlin Rose, who convinced shipping companies that lime juice administered in this form to seamen could prevent scurvy. Thus, the mixture's notoriety spread through worldwide ports.

RHUM: Originating in the Caribbean about 1600, rhum is thought to have been made first by the Spanish after Columbus brought sugar cane to the West Indies from the Azores.

This distilled liquor, sometimes aged, is

part of the sugar crop. After sugar cane is boiled down, the crystallized liquid becomes sugar itself. What remains is dealt with in 2 ways: either treated to become molasses, or else fermented, distilled & aged to produce rum. Though some believe that the name derives from *succharum,* the Latin for "sugar," it first appeared in 1654. By 1657, rhum was being produced in New England, then shipped to Europe.

In 1745, British Admiral Edward Vernon (whose nick-name was "Old Grog") tried to prevent scurvy among the members of his crew by prescribing a ration of rum, water, and sometimes citrus juices or spices in place of their usual ration of beer. This continued not only in the British Navy, but also in the U.S. Navy after the Revolution. Lincoln ended the practice in 1862; however, the Confederate Navy continued it into the Civil War. Not until 1970 did the British bring it to an end, more than 200 years after its beginnings.

Prior to the rise of Castro in Cuba, most of the rhum consumed in the U.S. came from that island just 90 miles south of Key West. After the revolution, though, most makers of rhum moved south and east to Puerto Rico; however, that is not the only Caribbean island to excel in this product.

Generally, the lighter the rum, the higher the proof, and the Virgin Islands and Puerto Rico produce light, dry rums. In Puerto Rico, the lightest ("white label" or *carta blanca*) are 80 proof, aged from 2-5 years, mixed in DAIQUIRIs and SOURs; the golden (gold label or *carta d'oro*) are 80 proof, aged 5-8 years, drunk like a WHISKEY on-the-rocks or in highballs, CUBA LIBREs, or COLLINS. Hawaii produces a soft, light rum; Haitian rhum is heavy flavored, but smooth. Barbados rhum ranks between the lighter rums of Puerto Rico and the darker rums of Jamaica; Bermuda rum, as well as that from the banks of the Demerara River in Guyana, is also lighter than Jamaican rum,

but just as assertive. By far, the rhum of Jamaica is the most pungent. Dark and tasting of molasses, these "black rums" are not at all thick; they just seem so.

And though some might place a premium upon the potent 151 proof stuff, it is best left to only the hardiest of rhum drinkers. True connoisseurs seek out *añejo* ("ancient") rhum aged some 15 years to become a smooth and mellow liquor, best savored like a fine brandy.

151 RHUM contains 75.5% alcohol, which is known as an "overproof" rhum. As such, this is not only a highly flammable dark rhum, but also one whose vapors at room temperature make it very aromatic.

RYE WHISKEY: Also AMERICAN WHISKEY.

S

SABRA: Liqueur produced from oranges with slight chocolate flavor. (Israel)

ST. RAPHAËL: Wine-based APÉRITIF with quinine.

SAMBUCA: Liqueur with licorice flavor. (Italy)

SANGAREE: Tall, sweet mixed drink topped with nutmeg.

SHOOTER: Straight drink poured from the bottle directly into the glass; mixed drink taken in a single gulp.

SIMPLE SYRUP: Also SUGAR SYRUP

To make your own:
2 cups Sugar
1 cup Water

Add Sugar to Water in a small saucepan. Stir until sugar has dissolved.
Bring the mixture to a simmer and continue stirring over heat for 10 minutes.
Pour into heatproof container, cover, and refrigerate. Keeps indefinitely.

SLING: Either whiskey or gin or brandy mixed with lemon juice, sugar, and soda water. Served in a tall glass, hot or cold.

SLIVOVITZ: Brandy from plums.

SLOE GIN: Liqueur from sloe berries steeped in gin.

SODA: See CLUB SODA

SOUR: Tart mixed drink that contains a combination of SOUR MIX with LIQUOR or LIQUEUR.

SOUR GLASS: Wide-mouthed, tapered stemware with a capacity of 5 or 6 ounces which will hold about 4 ounces of spirit, citrus juice, and sugar plus ice.

SOUR MIX: Combination of LEMON juice, LIME juice, and sugar used to create various mixed drinks.

To make your own:
Juice of 4 Lemons
Juice of 2 Limes
18 oz. Distilled Water
¼ cup Sugar
1 Egg White **

** *Due to the slight risk of Salmonella or other food-borne illness, I always must recommend caution in consuming raw egg whites. To reduce this risk, always use only clean, fresh, grade A or AA eggs that have been properly refrigerated. Be certain that their shells have remained intact and avoid contact between the yolks or whites and the shell.*

Fill your blender with the ingredients.
Blend at low speed to dissolve sugar.
Pour into covered container and keep refrigerated.
Use within 7-10 days.
Shake well before each use.

SOUTHERN COMFORT: Brand name liqueur of high proof from peaches, PEACH LIQUEUR, and BOURBON.

STRAWBERRY LIQUEUR: Liqueur produced from strawberries. See FRAISES.

STREGA: Liqueur produced from sweet herbs and spices. (Italy)

SUGAR SYRUP: See SIMPLE SYRUP

SWEDISH PUNSCH: Liquor with rhum base and citrus flavor.

T

TENNESSEE WHISKEY: American whiskey filtered through a layer of maple charcoal by the Lincoln County Process before being aged in wooden casks. The original Jack Daniel's Distillery was located in Lincoln County Tennessee.

TEQUILA: In the Tequila district of Mexico, they are fond of a plant with the Latin name *Agave tequilana;* however, out in the foothills of the Sierra Madre, they know this *agave* as a relative of the cactus the Spanish call *maguey.* Though the stem of this succulent plant has all the appearances of an out-sized pineapple, its fruit yields sap, *aguamiel* ("honey water") used in producing two distinct potions: fermented, it becomes *madre pulque,* a variation of beer that tastes like sour milk and drives folks *loco;* fermented and distilled, it becomes *vino mezcal,* which is what we know as tequila. Because this is fermented, then distilled, tequilla is technically a BRANDY.

Premium tequila is bottled in Mexico. Clear tequila bottled right from the still is termed *blanco* and sold as "white" or "silver." "Gold" tequila that derives its pale amber color from caramel is termed *joven abocado.* A tequila aged in oak from 2 to 12 months is termed *reposado* or "rested." And anything aged in oak beyond that is termed *añejo,* "aged."

TIA MARIA: Liqueur with coffee flavor produced from Jamaican Blue Mountain coffee. (Jamaica)

TONIC WATER: Carbonated water flavored with LEMON, LIME, and QUININE.

TRIPLE SEC: Liqueur produced from skins of CURAÇAO oranges, redistilled until clear. See also COINTREAU, CURAÇAO.

TWIST: Making twists requires a clean cutting board, a sharp knife, a clean spoon, rubber gloves, and a piece of citrus: LEMON, LIME, ORANGE, or possibly GRAPEFRUIT.

To make Twists:

Cut off both ends off the citrus.

Along one side, make a cut in the peel of the citrus, from end to end. Be careful to cut only through the peel.

With the spoon, remove the pulp of the fruit from the center of the citrus.

Reserve the pulp for making juice, but roll the peel into a tight cylinder.

Slice the rolled citrus peel into strips about a quarter-inch wide.

Twist each strip into a corkscrew shape before using.

Rub the rim of the glass with the rind, then hook the twist on the rim to garnish.

TUACA: Liqueur with BRANDY base, citrus flavors, and milk. (Italy) Also known as MILK BRANDY.

V

VANDERMINT: Liqueur with mint and chocolate flavors. (Holland)

VERMOUTH: APÉRITIF with aromatic herbs and spices, such as cinnamon, camomille, gentian, angelica root, and quinine. Produced in sweet and dry varieties, the best are from Italy and France; however, the word itself comes from the German *Wermut,* for "wormwood," a bitter, aromatic herb once used as a tonic to rid the human intestines of worms. This same herb was used in making this wine.

VIRGIN: Any mixed drink from which the acohol has been intentionally omitted.

VODKA: At the end of the 10th century, the Poles were producing *zhizennia voda* ("water of life"). In the 12th century,

Russians called it *vodka* ("little water").

By legal definition in the U.S., a distilled liquor of high proof "without distinctive character, aroma, or taste." Distilled from a fermented mash of water, grain, and yeast, this liquor is not aged. Connoisseurs can detect the subtle differences among Russian and Scandinavian distillers, but most rely upon either its lack of taste, or else some flavor from the infusion with fruits or peppers. Thus, a pepper vodka for a CAJUN MARTINI can be created simply by placing 2 or 3 whole jalapeño peppers into a bottle of quality vodka.

W

WHISKEY: Here's that phrase again: "water of life." In Gaelic, that's *uisgebeatha,* and that eventually led us to our own version of the word. Outside the U.S., they drop the *e* in the spelling; however, this does nothing to stop it from becoming the predominant hard liquor consumed in the States: something in the area of 80%.

Though not all whiskeys do taste alike, they all are produced from grains. It is this selection of grain, along with the distilling method and the aging process that creates a particular taste. *Blended* whiskey, such as RYE, contains 20-30% *straight* whiskey combined with neutral spirits. *Blends* are 2 or 3 *straight* whiskeys selected for strength, mellowness, aroma, and flavors. SCOTCH whiskey often blends up to 30 different *straight* whiskeys to create flavors.

WILD TURKEY: Liqueur with BOURBON base and light flavors of spice.

WINE: Fermented juice of grapes; however, other juices can also be used.

Y

YUKON JACK: Liqueur with Canadian-whisky base and flavors of citrus and herbs.

OLAF NORDSTROM is a bartender/fisherman/carpenter/philosopher/substitute teacher/raconteur/and mariner who also has written THE MARGARITAVILLE™ COOKBOOK, THINGS YOU KNOW BY HEART: 1001 QUESTIONS FROM THE SONGS OF JIMMY BUFFETT, and THE ESSENTIAL BOOK OF TEQUILA. He always claims to be working on A BARFLY'S GUIDE TO KEY WEST. In addition, he has been a holder of THE GUINNESS BOOK OF RECORDS™, off and on, since 1971.

Living aboard *SV Victorious Egret*, he summers on the Vineyard Sound and winters on Crab Key. Whatever the latitude, he cooks, eats, drinks, fishes, sails, reads, writes, and spends as little time working as necessary. In short, he is not only a man who gave up his own name, but also the person your parents warned you about.

WWW.MARGAREADER.COM

Made in the USA
Charleston, SC
27 June 2014